All about Guard Dogs
and Their Training

Also by John Cree

TRAINING THE GERMAN SHEPHERD DOG (ALSATIAN)
NOSEWORK FOR DOGS
ALL ABOUT TRAINING THE FAMILY DOG

All about Guard Dogs and Their Training

JOHN CREE

PELHAM BOOKS

First published in Great Britain by
PELHAM BOOKS LTD
27 Wrights Lane
London W8 5TZ
1986. Reprinted 1987

British Library Cataloguing in Publication Data
Cree, John
    All about guard dogs and their training.
    1. Watchdogs—Training
    I. Title
    636.7'0886   SF428.8

ISBN 0-7207-1661-6

Typeset by Sunrise Setting, Torquay, Devon
Printed and bound in Great Britain by
Butler and Tanner Limited, Frome, Somerset

To Colin and Bill,
two sons-in-law who have put
theory into practice

Contents

List of Illustrations   11
Preface   15
Acknowledgements   16
Abbreviations   17

CHAPTER 1 – *THE VARIATION IN GUARDING DUTIES*   19
   Introduction   19
   Domestic situations   20
   Operational situations   21
   The warning dog   23
   The deterrent   23
   The protector   25

CHAPTER 2 – *TYPES OF DOG FOR DIFFERENT DUTIES*   26
   Introduction   26
   Canine characteristics   26
   Temperament   27
   Character   27
   The senses   27
   Physique and stature   29
   Dog's reactions and development of situations   30
   Choice of dog   37
   The sex of the dog   42

CHAPTER 3 – *MORAL RESPONSIBILITIES*   43
   Introduction   43
   Handler control   43
   Failure to control   46
   Dangers of manwork   49
   Domestic guard dogs   51
   Breeders' responsibilities   51
   Operational guard dogs   53
   'Excellent guard dogs on offer'   54
   Gate signs   56

CHAPTER 4 – *LEGAL RESPONSIBILITIES*   61
    Introduction   61
    The domestic scene   61
    The operational scene   62
    Guard Dogs Act 1975   64

CHAPTER 5 – *CONTROL TRAINING*   67
    Introduction   67
    Basic principles   69
    The art of communication   69
    Basic equipment   71
    Control exercises   74
       Gaining your dog's attention   74
       To come back when called   75
       Loose lead walking   77
       The stay exercises   80

CHAPTER 6 – *TRAINING FOR GUARDING DUTIES*   88
    Introduction   88
    An awareness and indication of a presence   90
    To speak when required   91
    Acceptance of a presence   93
    Objection to a presence   94
    Detecting a presence and indicating the source 95
    Maintaining contact and keeping an intruder at bay 100

CHAPTER 7 – *TRAINING FOR PROTECTION DUTIES*   103
    Self defence and prevention of escape   103
    Controlled aggression   104
    The uninterested dog   111
    On to the arm   112
    Protection equipment   113
    Physical agitation and tests of courage   114
    Searching and disarming a criminal   116
    The chase or pursuit and detention   117
    Escorting the criminal   120
    Your dog and the gun   120
    Food refusal   122

CHAPTER 8 – *QUARTERING FOR A HIDDEN PERSON*   124
    Introduction   124
    To quarter in the open   125
    Building searches   128

CHAPTER 9 – *GUARDING AND PROTECTION VERSATILITY*
                                                    130
    Introduction   130
    Quartering situations   130
    Agility   131
    Protection work   132
    Working Trials   133

Appendix   135

Index   150

List of Illustrations

A park security dog finds a lost and injured child.   22

This reaction should have been an adequate deterrent.   24

Tara (Dunmonaidh Pixie C.D.Ex.) acts as protector.   24

A clatter should alert any handler but the dog's reaction is unmistakable.   28

Nose held high indicates a hidden party.   28

The Collie eye stares out a climbing youth.   29

Caro (Tanfield Atholl of Ardfern C.D.Ex. U.D.Ex. W.D.Ex. T.D.Ex.) – a German Shepherd Dog of physique and stature.   30

Corrie (Woodland Stroller) indicates in a domestic situation.   31

Corrie welcomes an accepted visitor.   32

Sabre (Sabre Molyneaux) gives his handler full backing.   33

Sabre now accepts a more stable situation.   34

Fonz (Callan's Son of Callanway C.D.Ex. U.D.Ex. W.D.Ex. T.D.Ex. P.D.Ex.) keeps an intruder at bay.   34

Rio (W.T.Ch. Lynrio's Domingo C.D.Ex. U.D.Ex. W.D.Ex. T.D.Ex. P.D.Ex.) takes positive action to prevent an escape.   35

Sabre reacts to a threatening attitude.   36

A Rhodesian Ridgeback.   37

A Rottweiler (Herburger Rio Grande – M.R.C. Temperament tested – Excellent).   39

What future for this G.S.D. puppy? (Pittrothie Shabbes Goy)   39

Three Belgian Shepherd Breeds:

A Tervueren (Tiffany Tis me)   40

A Malinois (Sabrefield Did You Call Tiffany)   40

A Groenendael (Viroflay Jeanette C.D.Ex. U.D.Ex. W.D.Ex. T.D.Ex.)   41

Chisum (Vikkas Emissary) in training for working trials:

Heelwork.   44

Tracking.   44

Protection.   45

A Rottweiler puppy with an expression of innocence and destined to become Barbadian Ch. Herburger Count Rasputin.   52

Gate signs come in many forms but wording must be chosen with care.   56–60

Sabre can accept an innocent child but will attack as necessary.   68

Hands and voice maintain Corrie's attention.   70

A combi-collar – also a strong trigger clip on lead.   71

Correct fitting of check chain, but demonstrated on left wrist.   72

Incorrect fitting of check chain, will not slacken when released.   72

Police style lead with trigger clip at each end and suitably placed rings to create varying lengths.   73

All-in-one leather lead and collar; the silent application is ideal for night work.   73

Corrie's handler moves to tap his hindquarters to obtain an immediate response.   74

Hand and body actions help to achieve a responsive recall.   77

First stage in lead holding during training.   78

Holding lead correctly in right hand with left hand ready for action as required.   79

Physically assisting Blue (Jaelr Royale C.D.Ex.) into sit position.   82

Completing the assisted sit.   83

Ensuring a contented and stable stay at the sit.   83

The three movements from the sit to down position. (Vikkas Electra of Ardfern C.D.Ex. U.D.Ex.)   84–5

Shadowsquad Callum of Ardfern C.D.Ex. U.D.Ex. W.D.Ex. P.D.Ex.   87

With check chain in hand Caro is induced to speak.   92

Detecting and indicating requires versatility and experience.   96

Caro has detected an intruder and is indicating his presence.   97

Chisum watches the intruder go into hiding . . .   98

. . . then follows up with purpose.   99

Caro turns to his handler and takes his attention from the intruder.   100

Caro ensures that the intruder will not move.   101

The full protection suit.   103

Chisum training with the sack.   105–6

Caro being used to entice youngsters to take an interest.   106

Tara's determination to hold on.   108

The use of a sailcloth dummy to induce a good bite.   109

Encouraging a good determined bite without the use of a 'criminal'.   110

A training 'criminal' prepares his arm.   112

The value of a well-padded sleeve as Rio takes a bite.   113

The gentle kick.   114

Bringing an intruder into the open.   116

Searching an intruder for weapons.   117

Fonz catches a running 'criminal'.   118
Pattern for quartering to find a missing person or concealed intruder.
  126
A Dobermann (Koriston Pewter Strike of Doberean C.D.Ex. U.D.Ex.
  W.D.Ex. T.D.Ex.) taking the long and clear jumps.   131–2
Caro takes the scale jump.   133

Preface

Some years ago I was asked to write a book on the subject of guard dog training. The answer at that time was a very definite NO. I considered this to be a very dangerous subject and I did not want to encourage dog owners into a field which could well ruin a well-behaved canine character.

However, situations change with time; with concern I watch and listen to the number of people who encourage their dogs to guard, without any understanding of the dangers or the need for control. I also view with concern the so-called 'trainers' who take good money from the unsuspecting public and proceed to create unreliable and dangerous dogs. There are some good and reputable dog trainers who have the knowledge and a responsible attitude to guard dog training. These trainers are very selective and treasure their reputation. They probably turn away more custom than they accept as a matter of responsible selection.

When I was again asked to write a book on this subject, I thought long and hard; then realised that many people require guidance and protection. I hope this publication achieves that objective and feel that if any reader decides against drawing on his dog's protective instincts as a result of my writings, this book will have served another useful purpose.

John Cree

Acknowledgements

Writing a book on such a delicate and emotive subject is not easy. A correct balance of aggressive attitudes with a keen sense of responsibility is all important. To achieve this the help and guidance of very knowledgeable people in their own fields made this book possible.

Legal advice was gratefully received from John Worland and Colin Ball, whilst the article from Mrs Rosalie Hughes of Herburger Rottweilers, which was originally published in *Dog Owner's Gazette*, was ideally suited to the chapter on Moral Responsibilities. The various photographic situations required the assistance of very enthusiastic helpers and my thanks must go to Bill and Joyce Rae, Alan Davie, Eric Roberts of Callanway, Ernie Fisher, Ian Griffiths, Drew Fleming and David Christie for their efforts.

Charles Allen of Birdbook kindly supplied a selection of his gate signs and Doris Allan has again come to my assistance with her artistic ability by producing some very realistic sketches. Irene, my wife, has also played her usual role in vetting and typing the manuscript and has helped in so many other ways to ensure that this work could go into print.

Photograph credits

The photographs were taken by the author except for the following which were gratefully received from various quarters (where known the names of the actual photographers are given in italics): *Jack Oliver*, page 30; John Middleweek, 35 and 113; Rosalie Hughes/*Diane Pearce*, 39; Jean Fry, 41; Rosalie Hughes, 52; Alan Whyte, 87; Jean Faulks/*Frank W. Paterson*, 131 and 132; Essex County Newspapers Ltd, 132.

Abbreviations

C.D.	Companion Dog
Ch.	Champion
Ex.	Excellent
G.S.D.	German Shepherd Dog
P.D.	Police Dog
Sch.H.I, II, III	Schutzhund (Guard or Defence Dog)
T.D.	Tracker Dog
U.D.	Utility Dog
W.D.	Working Dog
W.T.	Working Trials

1 The Variation in Guarding Duties

Introduction

The guarding duties and situations which involve a dog can vary considerably: the home, the factory or the game reserve are but three examples where dogs can be used for guardwork.

A dog which barks because of an unusual noise, the whiff of an unexpected scent or the feel of vibrations from unexpected movements, can be an ideal watch dog in many situations. A dog which threatens aggression will certainly make most unwelcome visitors think twice about giving trouble, and a dog which is trained for absolute protection will attend to the few intruders who do not have the wisdom to know better.

The types of situations for which guard dogs can be used can be broken down into two basic categories:

(a) DOMESTIC – e.g. the pet which may be expected to give some sort of warning that a visitor is at hand, and the dog which will act as a good deterrent against any threats of physical violence.
(b) OPERATIONAL – e.g. the dog which can be used to detect or deter an intending intruder, ranging to the dog which will stop and contain an escaping party who has been considered to have committed a detainable crime.

The requirements from a dog can also vary considerably and this certainly effects the choice and training of the dog, and the responsibility of ownership. These requirements can be broadly given as:

(1) The dog which will give WARNING.
(2) The dog which will act as a DETERRENT.
(3) The dog which will be PROTECTIVE of person and property.

Each of these roles cannot be completely separated from the others and it is easy to move from one to another without a full realisation of the change. Certain dogs such as Dobermanns, German Shepherds and the like, which will give warning will certainly act as a very strong deterrent, whereas a Papillon or a Chihuahua will only deter to the degree of an electric alarm system. On the other hand, a dog which is expected to act as a deterrent may well take up a very protective role, or even an offensive posture.

In other words, the three basic requirements are very closely linked together and when one particular requirement is the objective the effect on the others must be given due consideration.

Domestic situations

For centuries various communities and populations have used dogs to warn off and attack animal or human predators. The guarding of livestock was, and still is, an important function of our canine friends within certain environments. Many of our shepherding breeds have been developed from dogs which were used to protect flocks of sheep or herds of cattle.

Today, merely keeping a dog at home is enough to warn off the majority of intending intruders. Of course, if your dog is the friendliest creature in the neighbourhood, welcoming any visitor at any time, even during your absence, canvassers or trades callers will soon realise that he is no deterrent at all and this would soon become common knowledge. However, most dogs in the home will give some sort of indication that a 'visitor' is approaching.

I remember one occasion when a friend left the key of her house with a neighbour when she had to go out one afternoon. A tradesman was due to carry out some minor repairs and the neighbour agreed to stay with him until it was completed. However, the tradesman refused to enter the house when he heard the family pet barking from within. The owner's harmless Miniature Dachshund was rightly putting on his guard dog act and no amount of convincing would induce the tradesman to go in.

Unauthorised intruders are generally more sceptical about entering a home with a noisy dog around. Even a dog kennelled at the far end of the garden is likely to give voice and this can be enough to make intruders think again and look for easier pickings in a dogless home.

One frequently hears of cars being stolen these days but rarely of one which was left with a dog to look after it. However, I do recall one dog owner some years ago who left his estate car parked in the street. The back seat was down and his German Shepherd was left sleeping behind the driver's seat. On returning to his car he found that the vehicle had gone, but a glance down the road revealed its presence, badly parked, about one hundred yards or so from the original parking spot. On reaching his car he found everything in order with his dog wide awake and alert, but there was a fair amount of blood around the driver's seat.

It would appear that the thief had not noticed the sleeping dog and the starting of the engine probably brought the German Shepherd to life. Finding that his master was not at the wheel, the dog acted in a very positive and effective manner.

Many caravan tourists are also dog owners who enjoy the company of their pets on holiday. The caravan becomes the home for the holiday period and the presence of the family dog can act as a warning against night prowlers intent on some mischief.

A walk in the country or out in the dark can be enjoyed with complete confidence when accompanied by a suitable dog. This applies particularly to women.

In the main, dogs kept in a domestic situation are principally used as warning dogs, and thus will also serve as a deterrent, but the need for a protective dog is quite another matter although there may be occasions when one is advisable. The requirement to train a dog to take the initiative and apply an aggressive outlook should be considered with reservations.

Operational situations

Although this book is not intended to cover the full requirements of an operational police dog or a dog performing specialised security tasks within, say, a government department, the duties, selection and training for any working guard dog are similar in many respects.

Under the heading 'operational' there are a variety of situations where dogs can be used as guards, on commercial premises or estates, and also in city or country parks.

The type of commercial premises seeking the additional security a dog can provide varies tremendously: an out-of-the-way petrol-filling station owner may feel less vulnerable with a suitably conditioned dog on the premises; a licensed hotel owner may wish to discourage night intruders with a desire for easy drink or cash; or a shop owner whose house is attached to his business premises may have greater peace of mind with an alert dog in the building.

In many circumstances a dog may be expected to mix with the public during normal working hours but be on guard when most people are bedded for the night.

A security dog in attendance with a watchman or security guard when patrolling within a factory, warehouse or shopping complex will act as an extremely strong deterrent especially when it is known that the dog and handler have been trained for all the requirements of such a duty.

Under these circumstances a dog can indicate the presence of an intruder and pinpoint the exact location, no matter how well this uninvited guest has hidden himself. The dog can ensure the physical safety of his handler and also chase and restrain the intruder if the occasion is serious enough to warrant such drastic action.

A gamekeeper or water bailiff may well be required to patrol his beat as a deterrent against poachers, and on occasions he may find it necessary to protect himself against attack. If caught, a poacher can have all his equipment confiscated by law, and this can include his mode of transport, so poachers can be rather desperate characters and may well use force to

A park security dog finds a lost and injured child

avoid being apprehended. In these circumstances a good, strong, courageous dog can be a gamekeeper's or water bailiff's saviour.

A park security dog may well be required to carry out the full requirements of a working police dog, but within the confines of his patrolling area, and in a country park this can be quite extensive.

The parks dog may be expected to stop a bag snatcher one minute then hunt for a missing child the next. He may be required to subdue a group of young hooligans on a spree of vandalising, deter the indecent exposure maniacs, yet remain passive and friendly whilst some innocent party is looking to the handler for assistance.

The competitive field of working trials gives an opportunity for the civilian dog owner to train for a routine which is very similar to that of the working police dog.

My previous books, *Training the German Shepherd Dog* and *Nosework for Dogs*, cover the training requirements for working trials under the Kennel Club Regulations with the exception of the patrol group of exercises for the police dog stake.

These dogs must be safe and reliable with the versatility to do their job properly. The principal training routines in this book will cover the requirements for such dogs.

The warning dog

Giving a warning is a very natural action for most dogs. However, a certain amount of training may still be required. Dogs can give warnings in many different ways and these can vary according to the situation.

For example: a house dog may bark when somebody approaches his home; alternatively he may wait until the door bell rings; or he may wait until the door has opened and then bark or growl at the visitor. Only in the first case is he acting as a warning dog; in the other two instances he is acting as a deterrent.

On the other hand, a dog may become excited at the approach of a visitor and although this may be a sign of friendship towards the stranger it is also a warning of somebody's arrival. If the dog is of a nervous disposition the 'warning' reactions can be attributed to this fault in his breeding or upbringing.

In the car a dog may respond in exactly the same way as he does in the home, but a dog which welcomes an approaching visitor to the house may well set out to defend 'his' car in a most aggressive manner.

Whilst out for a walk a dog is unlikely to give voice as a warning of somebody approaching – in this situation a noisy bark would be quite unacceptable. However, most dogs do give some form of indication. The ears may become alert or the head may come up to sniff the scent which would help him to determine the source and origin. He may stand still for a second or two, listening or sniffing, before reacting in a more positive manner, but he may, rightly or wrongly, decide that the presence of the stranger is of no consequence. These are all signals whose value can be lost if they go unnoticed due to our own inattentiveness or pre-occupation.

The deterrent

The mere presence of a dog, whether it gives an obvious warning or not, is a deterrent to some extent. Many a burglar will not entertain a house as his objective if a dog is known to live within – it is too risky. Others with a certain understanding of dogs and a knowledge of particular animals, may well use that background to their advantage and will not be put off by the dog in question.

Ownership of certain breeds which are renowned for their guarding instincts can ensure that the risks of interference are minimal, either when at home or out for a walk, but again a party with an understanding of the breed or a knowledge of a particular dog's likely reaction can nullify any security which can be felt by the dog's presence.

However, the knowledge that a dog can *protect* or is likely to feel provoked into making an attack will certainly act as a very effective deterrent.

TOP This reaction should have been an adequate deterrent.
BOTTOM Tara (Dunmonaidh Pixie C.D.Ex.) acts as protector

The protector

This is a dog which looks as if he will assert his authority when certain situations develop. He will also protect by means of physical aggression when circumstances reach a state of open hostility on the part of the intruder against person or property.

Although the dog which is expected or trained to be a protector should rarely, if ever, be asked to apply physical aggression, it may well be necessary to train for this situation to ensure that full control can be attained. This will be more fully discussed in the appropriate parts of the text.

Protection work is an extremely sensitive area in the world of guard dogs. *The requirements and responsibilities must be given serious consideration before any attempt is made to draw on a dog's protective instincts.*

2 Types of Dog for Different Duties

Introduction

Each dog can have his own role to play in the guard-dog world. Every single dog can act as a warning dog or watch dog. Most dogs can also act as a deterrent to some extent under circumstances which suit the particular dog, although few can act as a strong deterrent under the most stressful conditions. The ultimate in guarding duties is protecting, where a dog must act not only as a warning and a deterrent, but also be prepared to defend his handler with his life.

The qualities required in a dog will change and become more exacting as we go up the scale from the simple domestic pet which will take note of an approaching visitor to the defender of life and limb.

The various guarding functions make demands on differing canine characteristics which are affected by selection, upbringing, training and control. Knowledge of these different characteristics can help you to appreciate the dog's requirements to meet the various situations.

Canine characteristics

A dog's nature and abilities are the result of a combination of temperament, character and the strengths of his various senses. This is a very complex business and when these factors are integrated with the dog's environment the complexity is subsequently increased.

A dog's reactions are determined by his character and the situation of the moment. Although reactions change with circumstances the basic character of the dog remains unaltered. The experience gained, however, may modify future reactions. One dog may have a 'happy-go-lucky' attitude most of the time but could break down under pressure. One unhappy experience of this pressure may well affect his outlook the next time the pressure is applied – the basic character of the dog has not changed although his future reactions will. Another dog may appear to have a well-balanced approach to life but can become extremely aggressive when certain stressful situations arise. This may not be due to a defect in his character but the result of some previous experience. However, by looking at the broad spectrum of canine actions and reactions, it is possible to place a dog into a definite category within the band of canine characteristics.

Temperament

Some dogs can be considered as being friendly; some may be overfriendly and with everybody – they may even welcome a burglar into their homes and leave with him if the burglar so chose. Others can be more particular with the distribution of their affection and may even be considered to be aloof to all except the family circle and the closest of family friends.

Aggressiveness without any apparent reason can be another side of a dog's temperament although a fuller knowledge of his background may indicate that the problem does not have a genetic source, but could be due to a particular experience. However, aggression may be tied up with another possibility – nervousness.

Nervousness can show up in a number of ways, such as being shy or retiring to the degree that the dog cannot be approached by those outside the family circle without his wanting to hide or get out of the way. Such a situation may also bring out aggressiveness through the fear of being trapped. A nervous reaction can also account for attentiveness to the extent of showing an unnatural fear of sounds or unexpected movement.

Character

Character helps to fill in the picture which is affected by temperament. Alertness, observance and attentiveness are important factors. They can be combined with canine enthusiasm to create an atmosphere of readiness and dependability. Confidence, a calm self-assurance and the resilience to overcome any unexpected event can be taken as the basis for courage, which can give any handler a feeling of trust in his canine partner.

Tractability together with intelligence are factors which will help to turn a dog into a valuable asset within his environment.

The senses

The senses vary in strength from one breed to another and from one dog to another. The strengths are all part of the genetic make-up – they are inherited; but environment and training along with the dog's natural temperament and character can sharpen particular senses to obtain the maximum value from nature's contribution to life.

The senses of hearing and scenting are the principal features which give a dog advantages over man. These are the senses which are the basis of good guarding work.

A clatter should alert any handler but here the dog's reaction is unmistakable.

Nose held high indicates a hidden party.

The Collie eye stares out a climbing youth.

The sense of hearing is probably the most important of the senses and especially with the erect-eared dogs where sounds which cannot be picked up by the human ear will readily be heard by the dog.

The sense of smell is probably the most acute of a dog's senses and this enables him to pick up scents which are extremely faint and at a distance. However, this sense in itself is of no value if the wind is not in the right direction.

Sight is a sense which, with most breeds, does not compare too well with that of man. With the exception of the Gazehound group of breeds, which are extremely keen sighted, dogs have a tendency to be short-sighted and it may take a movement to attract their attention.

The sense of feel can also be invaluable: sensitivity to vibrations, particularly in a resting dog, can alert the other senses and the nose and the ears can then take over (these are the senses most likely to locate the source of the movement).

Physique and stature

Physique and stature may not be factors which affect the value of a warning dog, but the deterrent and protection aspects of guarding duties are governed by such features.

Caro (Tanfield Atholl of Ardfern C.D.Ex. U.D.Ex. W.D.Ex. T.D.Ex.) – a German Shepherd Dog of physique and stature

A breed of dog which looks the part has been developed with a purpose in mind and this generally includes a measure of guarding capabilities.

Dog's reactions and development of situations

The complete make-up of the dog, the combination of strengths and weaknesses, affects his every action and response. It is the circumstances of the moment which bring out his reactions. To understand desired reactions it is necessary to appreciate the principal developing situations within the world of dog guarding activities.

The situations which are used to illustrate guarding functions are based on the approach or presence of a person, be it authorised or not. Although the situations are developed to handle the warning, deterrent or protection of people and property from human intruders, in the protection of livestock from animal predators, such as chickens or lambs from a fox, the principle is as valid.

1. *Awareness of a presence*
Awareness brings out the alertness of a dog to situations which warrant his attention. It is surprising just how alert most dogs can be, even when they appear to be sleeping. They seem to be sensitive to vibrations and sound and either of these could bring the animal into a more alert state where other senses may be brought into action.

Temperament is a factor which could affect alertness, particularly in a dog which is of a shy or retiring nature. Dogs in this category tend to be on edge and thus more readily alert to a presence than a dog which is completely relaxed.

Dogs with a natural or encouraged aggressive streak also tend to be more alert, but this advantage – with a shy dog or an aggressive dog – can well become a handicap if there is a lack of control when matters develop to a more stressful point.

A dog of stable and unflappable temperament should act with sufficient alertness and will certainly be able to cope with natural developments.

2. *Indicating a presence*

This is the ability and desire to indicate a presence to a handler, say, when somebody is approaching, or the handler and dog are approaching a person, or a person is hiding in the vicinity.

Basic awareness of a presence will normally be sufficient to cause a noticeable reaction but the particular circumstances should create an appropriate and distinctive reaction from the dog.

The reaction to a visitor approaching the house during the day may be minimal and quite acceptable but a similar situation during the evening or at night should create a much more active response, making it perfectly

Corrie (Woodland Stroller) indicates in a domestic situation.

clear to the handler that there is a reason to take note. Barking would certainly be the most suitable active response.

Again, alertness and temperament are factors of the greatest influence and a dog with an unstable temperament will probably show the most natural and obvious indication of a presence. A nervous or aggressive dog is more likely to give voice than a dog of stable temperament and character which has not been encouraged or trained to react in a suitable manner.

However, this is the stage where any possible advantage in having a nervous or aggressive dog terminates.

3. *Acceptance of a presence*

This brings out the stability of canine character and the dog's ability to interpret the handler's approval of a visitor. The dog should become relaxed and accept the handler's judgment. A dog with a 'happy-go-lucky' attitude is likely to welcome any visitor so that any pretence at being a deterrent is lost, even if he barks to 'indicate' after showing an 'awareness'.

This is possibly the most suitable type of watchdog a household can

Corrie welcomes an accepted visitor.

have, one which will not cause any problems. A dog which is shy and reserved is unlikely to accept the presence of any visitor unless that visitor is well known to the dog. If this type of dog can just take himself off then there is no problem, but if he feels cornered he is likely to take up a defensive or aggressive stance. Because of this weakness in his temperament visitors will be few and far between.

The dog with an even temperament will be able to assess his handler's acceptance and although he may not welcome an unknown visitor, he will stay at hand without any indication of hostility.

4. *Objection to a presence*

A handler's reservations about a visitor or intruder should be acknowledged by the dog as cause for concern. The handler can be apprehensive and this should be interpreted by the dog who is expected to respond accordingly.

This requires a dog which is steady and loyal, self-assured and attentive of the presence. He should also be easily controlled if an exchange of words becomes heated.

Sabre (Sabre Molyneaux) gives his handler full backing.

The following is principally for the operational dog

5. *Detect a presence*

Detecting and locating an uninvited intruder is a very important aspect of security work. A person skulking in a dark doorway may be missed by a watchman or security guard but a dog will be aware of his presence through one of the senses already mentioned. The intruder may be hidden behind equipment, or even inside an open packing case, but the right type of dog

Sabre now accepts a more stable situation.

Fonz (Callan's Son of Callanway C.D.Ex. U.D.Ex. W.D.Ex. T.D.Ex. P.D.Ex.) keeps an intruder at bay.

with suitable training will certainly be able to indicate such a presence.

To be capable of detecting a presence a dog's senses must be at their sharpest with an attentiveness which has been brought to a peak through training and experience.

6. *Indicate the source*

This is the natural progression from detecting a presence where the dog is expected to 'home in' on the intruder and show an interest in the location.

The inquisitive side of canine character comes into the picture now, along with a determination to find the source of his interest. This may also require a steadiness of nerve and the physical ability to overcome obstacles which happen to be between the dog and the handler.

7. *Maintain contact with intruder*

The dog which will bark on discovering the location of an intruder will have the added advantage of being able to work at a distance from the handler and can let him know of his find.

To maintain constant contact with a hidden intruder requires determination together with enthusiasm and a measure of self-confidence on the part of the dog.

8. *Keeping an intruder at bay*

An attentive and preferably a barking dog which maintains contact will certainly make an intruder think twice about trying to make a quick exit.

Although self-confidence is a very important characteristic, a dog with an impressive physique and stature will pose more of a real threat to an intruder than will a small one.

Rio (W.T.Ch. Lynrio's Domingo C.D.Ex. U.D.Ex. W.D.Ex T.D.Ex. P.D.Ex.) takes positive action to prevent an escape.

9. *Preventing the escape of an intruder*

An intruder is unlikely to try to escape when found by a large and powerful dog which has the determination to maintain contact. However, the intruder may well size up the situation *before* the dog is close enough to detect his presence and may try to make a quick exit prior to discovery.

On such an occasion the dog may be required to give chase, catch and then detain the intruder until the handler arrives to take over.

A fast and agile dog with the resolution to pursue and stop an escaping intruder must respect the control of his handler in order to ensure that the situation is managed with the minimum of applied force.

10. *Self-defence and handler protection*
The intruder, when discovered, may attack the dog if the handler is not immediately at hand, or there could be an accomplice (or accomplices) who might attack the dog and his handler.

The dog must therefore be prepared to assess the situation and react in a manner which will minimise the possibility of injury to his handler and himself. At the same time he should remain in contact with at least one intruder.

Courage together with the physique and ability to attack are now very prominent requirements. However, the ability to apply self-control on the termination of hostilities is equally important. A dog of very balanced character is a necessity under such conditions.

Such, then, are the situations and the canine characteristics which are most suited to our various requirements. Some of the responses described will come naturally to a number of dogs. In many instances training will be

Sabre reacts to a threatening attitude.

carried out quite unconsciously by the handler, particularly with the domestic dog which is required only to give the desired warning as the situation demands. As the requirements which involve positive deterrent and protection aspects become more demanding, so the environment, training and control of the dog assume more importance.

This affects the choice of dog: the breed, selection within a breed and also the sex. These factors all combine to control the effectiveness for the functions we have in mind.

Choice of dog

There are many breeds to choose from, plus cross-breeds and mongrels to widen the choice.

As already mentioned any dog can act as a warning dog, be it a pure breed or a mixture of many breeds. Not all dogs will make a noise but many a quiet one can be taught to bark. The Basenji is, of course, an exception: it is listed as a barkless dog.

Most dogs can be a deterrent if the noise from, or the presence of, a dog is sufficient to deter an intending intruder, but to act as a *real* deterrent a dog must look the part or be a breed with a certain reputation. The dog does not require to be one of the large breeds; reputation alone, be it valid or not, can act as a strong deterrent. A Bull Terrier in the garden, with its reputation as a fighter, can act as an extremely strong deterrent for anybody wishing to enter. A Labrador Retriever is considered to be a big soft lump of a family dog but this reputation can be misleading. Having

A Rhodesian Ridgeback.

watched a few Labradors working in police dog trials it is evident that a well-trained Labrador with suitable breeding can be equally as effective as any of the more popular guard-dog breeds.

Examples of small breeds which can act as a strong deterrent would include the Wire-haired Fox Terrier and the Staffordshire Bull Terrier from the terrier group of breeds.

The diminutive Dachshund from the hound group can be a little devil and the possibility of nipped ankles has probably discouraged some would-be intruders. The Rhodesian Ridgeback certainly has the right ancestry, where strength of character for lion hunting was its prime requirement.

From the utility group of breeds the Bulldog still carries the reputation of the bull-baiting dogs and, although they may be the gentlest of animals, the sight of one can be quite sufficient to put someone off.

When looking at the toy or the gun-dog groups it is difficult to visualise the presence of any of these breeds acting as a strong deterrent, although the actions of individual specimens may well cause people to reconsider their plans.

The working group of breeds naturally carries the highest proportion of true present-day guarding dogs, and while some breeds within the group may not be considered for professional working duties, they could certainly act as a strong deterrent in the home. These include Mastiffs and Corgis. Mastiffs have the necessary physique and stature, while Corgis, because of their cattle-herding instincts and background, have the ability to quickly nip the heels of cattle and, therefore, a two-legged human substitute.

The German Shepherd dog (Alsatian) is probably the best known and the most popular of the guarding breeds. This breed has the attributes and versatility to cope with all the duties which can be asked of a warning, deterrent and protection dog. It is also the easiest to train and the most manageable in all circumstances.

There are, of course, German Shepherds which are completely unsuitable for guarding duties, which call upon the true characteristics of the breed. The result of mismatched parentage, an undesirable upbringing or an inadequate handler can create a Shepherd which will have a limited or unreliable effect.

The Dobermann is probably the sharpest and most attentive of breeds with an aggressiveness which, when properly applied, can earn him the reputation of the complete guarding dog. However, his independent nature can make him difficult to control so that special handling abilities are essential to ensure that he maintains a safe and reliable approach to his working life, especially when he is expected to mix with the general public. This dog has a lot to offer but in the wrong hands he can be a positive menace.

The Rottweiler is another breed which has much to offer as a guarding

A Rottweiler (Herburger
Rio Grande M.R.C.
Temperament tested –
Excellent)

What future for this
G.S.D. puppy?
(Pittrothie Shabbes Goy)

THIS PAGE AND OPPOSITE
Three Belgian Shepherd
breeds: RIGHT A
Tervueren (Tiffany 'Tis
Me)

A Malinois (Sabrefield
Did You Call Tiffany)

A Groenendael (Viroflay
Jeanette C.D.Ex.
U.D.Ex. W.D.Ex.
T.D.Ex.)

dog, with an ancestry which goes back to Roman fighting dogs. His size and weight can mislead one into thinking that he lacks speed and agility when in fact he is probably one of the most agile of breeds – a fit Rottweiler will most likely outstrip most of the other working breeds.

Although they appear at times to be as independent as the Dobermann, Rottweilers can be very affectionate towards their owners. Special handling ability is an essential if proper control is to be applied to this breed and any attempt to cover guarding duties would soon reveal handling weaknesses.

Of the more unusual breeds the Hovawart and the Bouvier Des Flandres can more than hold their own when trained for protection work.

German Shepherds, Dobermanns and Rottweilers are, however, the best known of our guarding dogs; they have the physique, the stature and the reputation. Together, these three factors can form the greatest deterrent of all.

However, it must be remembered that any breed of dog, with or without a reputation for guarding ability, can only carry out the required functions with safety if the breeding is within the particular breed standard and if the environment, control and training is satisfactory. Cross-breeds and mongrels also have their place in the guard-dog world but their qualities are more individualistic. Each dog will vary according to its ancestry; the inherited traits are much less predictable than those of a standard breed, and suitability can only be judged by studying the dog and his responses to various situations.

The sex of the dog

The sex of the dog can have a bearing on its attitude and effectiveness. It is recognised that bitches, because of their maternal instinct, are likely to be more alert and sharper than males of the same breed. Although this can be an attraction, it must be identified as a factor which will require control with a greater strength of character on the handler's part. With a domestic pet this may mean that each member of the family must be capable of applying the necessary control.

When it comes to security work with its attendant more advanced guarding duties, male dogs possess the desired physique and stature and are not bothered by heat seasons which can put a bitch out of action for a few weeks approximately every six months.

3 Moral Responsibilities

Introduction

All dog owners have to answer for the actions of their dogs, and the introduction of any form of guarding activities can only add to these responsibilities.

Dog owners are morally and legally bound to ensure that their dogs are completely safe under all circumstances. A dog which has been encouraged or trained to keep watch, guard, seek out or protect must be reliable. He may attack only as a means of defence and, like an attack by one person on another, the need for and severity of an attack may well be answerable in a court of law.

I do not think there is any need to try and determine the difference between moral and legal responsibilities. The law is there to ensure that moral standards are upheld.

Starting with the simplest level of guardwork 'Awareness of a Presence' (as described in Chapter 2), any barking, growling or other canine reaction which can be interpreted as the *first* stage in the development of aggression, must be controlled. It need not necessarily be stopped, but it must be controlled to ensure that there is no further development unless the situation demands a stronger reaction. When we step up the ladder of guarding activities to full protection work the responsibilities become greater, the control requirements become more important and the approach to training becomes more critical.

Handler control

This is a vital factor and must be given serious consideration. Most problems which arise through guarding functions are due to a handler's inability to control a particular situation. This may be due to a lack of knowledge, a failure to appreciate the dangers, or a lack of forcefulness to match the dog's strength and desire to extend a situation. The more demanding the requirements from a dog, the greater is the necessity to achieve absolute control and instant obedience.

Handlers must be resolute in their approach with a determination to control any development which brings out aggressive canine reactions.

A dog's attitude changes with situations and so must that of the handler. I find that in the competitive field of working trials I am working one dog but three canine personalities. These cover the three basic sections of work: nosework; control; and criminal or protection work.

Chisum (Vikkas Emissary) in training for working trials.

Heelwork.

Tracking.

Protection.

In the nosework section the dog is guided into controlling the situation. Whilst working the track he is the senior partner and the handler is completely dependent on the dog's ability – a cross or firm word from the handler is likely to distract the dog.

When working a control round, a degree of gentle firmness may well be required to get the best out of the dog. Handler and dog work as equal partners. However, the dog knows that the handler is applying a measure of control.

The biggest change takes place during the criminal working group of exercises and it is difficult to explain the true relationship between handler and dog. The handler must be the master, he must be in control, his commands must be instantly obeyed – and yet the dog must have confidence to act quite independently of him. The dog must be able to assess the situation and act with maximum resolution, but be prepared to stop on command. On these occasions the handler's voice may well be hard and uncompromising with a harshness which would flatten his dog at any other time, but during this work it will only bring the dog down from a 'high' and back on an even keel.

Criminal, or protection, work may be demanding on the dog but it is much more demanding on the handler.

Failure to control

I make no apology here for considering the matter of 'failure'. Anyone who is interested in the subject of this book should read about the failings of others before them so as not to repeat the errors of the past. One simply cannot afford to learn from one's own mistakes.

A dog bite is commonplace; it happens daily – children are bitten, postmen are bitten, joggers are good sporting targets for many a family dog when out for early morning exercise. Dog owners are taken to court with monotonous regularity, where they try to defend the actions of their innocent little, or large, pets.

Accidents can happen. Some victims ask for trouble by the way they tease a dog whilst they themselves are safely positioned, but it may be some innocent party who is caught out.

I have seen dogs being tormented into a vicious rage whilst alone in the owner's car, by youngsters and by adults with a juvenile mind. These instances cause accidents but the majority of bites are caused by the handler's failure to appreciate situations and the failure to maintain adequate control. There are, of course, many occasions when a dog is accused of an aggressive act – accused of biting – and, because of his breed, he is condemned by all as being guilty.

One such case illustrates this point. I was involved in a legal case as an 'expert witness' and duly reported the full situation in an article for the *GSD League Magazine* (this is the official journal of the German Shepherd Dog League of Great Britain). This article was written at the time when the breed was known as the Alsatian:

Give a Breed a Bad Name
I was in court recently as an 'expert witness', being called to the defence of an Alsatian who had been accused of 'having bitten a person and not being under proper control'.

I have always been aware of the undeserved reputation our breed has been given and by a minority of incidents, when we consider the number of Alsatians in the country.

It is quite probable that some owners deserve to finish up in court. Others, who genuinely look after and control their dogs, are unfortunate enough to find themselves unprepared for an unexpected situation, and we once again find that the breed is being damned for an incident that may not have been the fault of the dog.

This case is one which should be of interest to every owner of our breed; it is a case where there was almost a miscarriage of justice.

Ricky is a two-year-old dog of unknown breeding. His dam had been found by a local farmer; she was in pretty poor shape and heavily in whelp. The police were notified but nobody claimed her. The farmer kept the bitch, attended to the whelping and saw that the puppies had a good start in life.

A neighbouring friend, who owned some of the fields rented by the farmer, was given one of the puppies; this was Ricky.

Ricky was brought up in a country atmosphere; his home was situated on the edge of a small town in Scotland's industrial belt, he had full access to his master's property and would often accompany the neighbouring farmer on his rounds whilst he checked up on his cattle. When the farmer made for home Ricky would turn and make for his own residence. He was no trouble to anybody, never strayed from his own 'patch', but he did not meet a lot of strangers and did not have the opportunity to become fully socialised.

My first contact with Ricky's problem was by telephone when the owner's wife rang me one evening. She had read an article in our local paper about my book *Training the Alsatian* and wondered if I could help. Her story of the incident was briefly as follows.

One Sunday morning in September Ricky's owner took him for a walk through the fields and returned via the Market Garden some three hundred yards from home. As usual when out in the country Ricky was not on the lead although his owner always had it with him. They went into the Market Garden Shop and as his owner was coming away he opened the door whilst still chatting with the proprietor. Ricky bounded out in his usual manner and apparently ran down the path to jump up on another customer coming to the shop. The injured party claimed to have been bitten and his wife, who followed up the path after the incident, was near to hysterics.

The owner had now been charged and his solicitor had advised him to plead guilty. As he was convinced that the mark on the injured party's back was not a bite, the owner was not prepared to accept the 'had bitten' part of the charge, could I help?

I spent a December evening with Ricky and his owners, sitting in the lounge, listening, talking and watching. My main objective was to assess the dog, but I also had to assess the owners and determine whether they would respond to any comments or advice that I could contribute.

My conclusions were that Ricky was slightly nervous by nature and the part isolation of his upbringing with only a few real friends had made him a bit wary of strangers, but he was no biter. From the details I had been given the mark on the injured party's back was that of a toe nail; bearing in mind that most of Ricky's exercising was carried out on pasture his nails were quite long and we all know what toe nails can do when we play with our Alsatians.

The owner decided to contest the charge and instructed his solicitor that a plea of 'not guilty' be put forward.

I was then called to a meeting with the solicitor who gave me fuller details of the incident and he also noted my impression of the dog and his owners. He was now quite convinced that the dog did not bite and asked if I would be prepared to appear in court as an expert witness for the defence.

The District Magistrates' Court
The first witness to be called was the wife of the injured party. She stated that she was in the car some fifty yards away speaking to the children, then looked around to see this big Alsatian on her husband's back. She did not see anything prior to this and could not see the dog actually biting, but her

husband was doubled up in pain. The dog came away when called by the owner. She also stated that there was a hole, which turned out to be an indentation, on the back of her husband's denim jacket. On removing his clothing there was a weal about four inches long down his back just below the right shoulder blade. The skin was slightly broken about half way down. She stated emphatically that this was caused by a dog bite.

The injured party was then called. He stated that he was walking up the path towards the shop and was about eight yards from the door when it opened and the Alsatian came bounding out and made an attack straight for him. He turned and stepped off the path to avoid the dog but it hit him on the back and bit him. He did acknowledge that the dog returned immediately to his owner when called. He also said he was in great pain from the bite and on removing his jacket he could see three distinct indentations from the dog's teeth with score marks extending from these indentations.

When asked by the defence if he could have been mistaken and was it not the dog's feet that hit his back, the reply was that he was definitely bitten by the dog.

The proprietor of the Market Garden was called but she was unable to confirm the dog's actions. Being in the shop at the time she could not see anything but she did confirm that there were two weals on the injured party's back about two inches long and about three inches apart. She also stated that she had known Ricky since he was weeks old; he was very friendly and an attack would be completely out of character.

The police constable who was sent to charge Ricky's owner was then called and he made it perfectly clear that his meeting with the dog was a frightening experience. The dog kept coming at him, snarling and snapping, and he finally had to ask the owner to put his dog out of the room. According to the constable the owner had to give a number of commands before the dog would obey. Asked by the defence if he was afraid of Alsatians the constable said he was very frightened of them but this did not affect his judgment of the situation. His view was that this was a very dangerous animal.

The policewoman who accompanied the constable was then called into court. Her evidence was similar to her colleague's but she also stated that the dog had them cornered. She admitted that she too was frightened of Alsatians.

Listening to the evidence of the two police constables, this dog did not have a chance. Here were two independent witnesses, with no axe to grind, giving a fair assessment of this dog *as they saw him*.

Ricky's owner was then called to the witness box. He had opened the shop door but did not notice anybody coming up the path. He was still talking to the proprietor when Ricky went out. The first he realised anything was amiss was the shout from the injured party. The owner said he thought the dog was just being playful. He had never been aggressive to anybody; it was not in the dog's nature.

Whilst I was listening to the owner's evidence I wondered how often magistrates had sat through a similar description of the ideal dog who could do no wrong and in the eyes of the owner the accusation against his dog was completely out of character.

I was then called into the witness box and questioned by the counsel for the defence. The first question was: 'From the evidence given in court, did I think that the injured party had been bitten?' I commented on the evidence which stated that the weals on the back were three inches apart; they could not therefore have been caused by a single attack with teeth. The points of the canines were no more than two inches apart; also if a canine was responsible for a weal two to four inches in length the outer clothing would have been torn. My impression from the evidence given in court was that a dog bite was highly unlikely.

I was then asked by the counsel for the defence to describe the purpose and the effect of the various teeth in an Alsatian's mouth, the incisors, the canines, the premolars and the molars. My description seemed to impress the magistrates and I felt that the tide was turning in the dog's favour.

I was then asked to describe my first meeting with Ricky. I recounted the events of that evening when Ricky objected strongly to my visit. He barked but kept near his master. If I moved he backed away and barked, but he would occasionally venture forward to investigate this visitor who was ignoring him completely. I got up and took off my jerkin. Any movement I made resulted in Ricky making a frightened but noisy retreat. To my mind this dog would only attack if cornered. Before the evening was finished Ricky overcame his fear and in fact enjoyed a little bit of fun. We could have a tug of war, with my index finger hooked behind the dog's canines. This dog was no vicious biter.

I also mentioned to the court that I could well understand the feeling of the two PCs who had a natural fear of Alsatians. Their reactions were quite understandable but this was not the dog's fault.

The counsel for the prosecution's only question was to ask if my comment that a bite was highly unlikely meant that there was a possibility of a bite. My reply was that I could not visualise any circumstances where teeth could have caused the weals in question or the marks on the jacket, but that all the evidence pointed to the marks having been made by the dog's toe nails.

Council for the prosecution then faced the magistrates and requested that the words 'had bitten' be removed from the charge. This was accepted by the court and a Court Order was made to keep the dog under better control.

Ricky is no longer branded as a biter and is now enjoying the weekly training sessions at our local club.

Why did Ricky jump on this unsuspecting stranger in the first place? Nobody saw Ricky run at the man except the victim himself. Ricky may have thought it was somebody he knew. We shall never know.

One thing for sure, Ricky's owner is now more appreciative of the fear some people have of our breed. We can argue about this injustice but these fears must be recognised and they will remain so long as dogs like Ricky are dragged into court with misplaced accusations.

Dangers of manwork

The trained dog with an experienced handler can turn out to be a liability if the handler tries to be too clever. I would like to think that every security guard has received the appropriate training to handle the dog in his charge. There was a time when, in some organisations, handler training appeared to be minimal. A householder who takes on a professionally trained protection dog for domestic or personal protection, should also undergo proper training to handle such a dog correctly.

There are quite a number of German Shepherds being imported from Germany these days and, although these dogs are being purchased specifically for breeding and showing, they generally have working qualifications which include varying degrees of protection work. Certain breeders are keen to show off this aggressive ability and, from time to time, the results give rise to concern. I was asked by a breeder friend to write a piece on the subject and the resultant article was duly printed in the weekly paper *Our Dogs*. It is reproduced here and I would mention that it could, of course, apply to any of the working breeds.

German Shepherd Dogs – the dangers of manwork

I had a lengthy discussion with a breeder friend at Crufts on the subject of imported German dogs and their potential in manwork. It became apparent during our discussion that we were both very concerned about the reputation of our breed and the full realisation that this reputation depended on sensible ownership of all GSDs. It would appear from the stories one hears that, because some imported dogs have had manwork or guard training prior to leaving their native country, some owners or handlers are tending to show what their new charges can do without any appreciation of the dangerous circumstances they may be creating. I have no way of telling if these stories are true but our breed has suffered in the past through unwise ownership and the subsequent publicity. *We cannot afford any more of it.*

I have been asked, however, to make some comments on the dangers of inexperienced handlers venturing into the field of manwork or even elementary guard-dog training. Firstly, it must be stated that the only acceptable criterion is that a dog is absolutely safe *at all times*. He will only 'go in' when the situation is right and he will 'come out' immediately when called. The dog must be given the confidence to discern between right and wrong occasions to show his guarding or attacking instincts, and the handler must have the control to terminate these actions as required.

Imported dogs may well have been fully trained to defend or attack but a dog who is continually enticed to show his worth without being given a 'bite' will become frustrated and, in his own time, will take the law into his own hands, or should I say 'mouth'. The handler who is not accustomed to controlling a dog when he takes the 'bite' will find he has no control over the dog or respect from this dog during those vital few seconds. There is also a strong likelihood that the frustrated dog may take advantage of a situation whilst his handler is not to hand. Again, I hate to think of the consequences.

There can be no amateurs in this business; every handler and 'criminal' must apply a serious professional approach. Handling a guard or manwork dog requires specialised training and recognising a person as knowledgeable in the dog business is just not good enough. Some people think that training a dog for manwork is a 'closed shop'; it is considered to be very difficult to get a professional 'criminal' to help. The 'criminal' trains the dog and also the handler to react correctly, and no sensible 'criminal' is going to assist a person whom he thinks is unsuitable or a dog without a stable and reliable character.

I was taught in a very cautious school where the handlers had to prove a genuine interest and responsible control by qualifying in working trials before the 'criminals' would consider helping train the dog for the Police Dog Stake. These 'criminals' were not interested in training a dog and handler just to satisfy their own ego.

The need for my writing has arisen because of comments about the unwise handling of certain imported GSDs. As I said, 'I do not know the truth of the matter,' but this warning goes out to anybody who has an interest in the breed and is acting unwisely. In fact the warning could be noted by the owners of any breed, who are tempted to show the protective instincts of their dogs when they have not had the benefit of professional training.

★　★　★

Domestic guard dogs

There are occasions when a pet dog, particularly in the working breeds, is purposely trained to give his master personal and property protection. Such dogs may well be giving a similar service to that of the security dog which is earning his keep and this is quite in order as long as the owner fully appreciates his responsibilities.

However, many a dog owner – and again especially of the working breeds – readily claims that his canine companion is a guard dog. This can help to keep undesirables away, but it should be borne in mind that such claims may well prejudice the owner's case if a court action ensues after an aggressive canine act has been committed.

Breeders' responsibilities

Breeders, particularly of the popular guarding breeds, also have a responsibility. It is all too easy to sell a puppy or a young dog which is not going to make the grade in the show ring, by explaining to a prospective buyer how protective the breed can be. To encourage an intending dog owner who has no background in controlling a protective dog is sheer folly.

However, the majority of breeders are more responsible and realise that prospective owners require vetting and guidance in order to minimise the risk of placing their stock into unsuitable homes. Not every prospective buyer is honest and forthright in giving the true reason for buying a puppy and one such incident was duly published in the magazine the *Dog Owner's Gazette* and is reprinted here.

A Rottweiler puppy with an expression of innocence and destined to become Barbadian Ch. Herburger Count Rasputin.

JAKE'S STORY *by Rosalie Hughes*

Some three years ago we had an enquiry from a farmer for a Rottweiler puppy. He said that he wanted a dog for a companion for his mother who, it seemed, spent a lot of time on her own. A visit was arranged for an interview with us, and to see and meet the 'gang'. Our famous 'Herburger Vetting Interviews' usually last for at least two hours, during which we give information and advice on owning a Rottweiler, and ask a lot of in-depth questions as to the suitability of the prospective puppy buyer.

In this case, the interview came to a satisfactory conclusion and a date was arranged to collect the puppy. 'Jake', as the puppy was called, went to his new home when he was eleven weeks old and was already a very happy, bouncy 'Rottie' baby. We were informed a few weeks later that he had settled down well, and was eating as directed on the diet sheet supplied, so all was well at this stage. No more news came forth till approximately five months later, when we received a phone call from the farmer; he said he was rather disappointed with the pup, to which the question from me was the obvious one: Why? His answer came as a shock; he said the puppy – then only seven-and-a-half months old – was not vicious enough for him, and a friend, who was supposedly an ex-police dog handler, had tried to 'bait him up', but had given up as he said the pup would 'never turn'. When I asked why he required such a vicious dog, and not, as originally requested, a companion for his mother, more was revealed. It appeared that part of the farm which he rented was down to forty acres of strawberries which, during the season, were being raided at night by local yobbos from the nearby town. He said he needed a nasty vicious dog as a deterrent when he patrolled the farm at night. But that when the strawberry season finished, the dog had to revert to a placid companion.

With no more ado, I told him we were on our way over to him, some 160-mile round trip. The one thought on our minds was to get the puppy back. Thank goodness for the wonderful steady temperament of Jake. We arrived at the farm, where we were greeted by a happy well-grown pup. It was incredible that he still remembered us, but then most puppies do. He had been on a chain to try to bring out a nasty streak, as the marks around his neck showed, but Jake still remained the happy, loving puppy he should be at such a tender age. Basically he had been well cared for and was very obedient, and his then owner was fond of him. He admitted he had not been totally honest with us as to his real requirements of the dog, so he agreed to let us have the pup back. We put Jake in the car and started the journey home.

In the weeks that followed, we were able to assess Jake's temperament and to make sure that it had not been spoiled by the adverse 'training' he had received in his last home.

We had had Jake back with us for about two and a half months, when his present owner came into the picture.

Ron Blakeman, who owns the Bull Hotel, Horncastle, had lost his Great Dane at a ripe old age and was looking for another dog to replace him. He had been marvellous with the family and the customers, and used to take part in the famous Medieval Banquets held there.

We took Jake to the Bull to meet Ron, his wife Sandie and their three children, the youngest being only a few months old. During the next two weeks, Jake made a number of visits to his new family, firstly for half an hour, then two hours, half a day, and finally he stayed for good. He settled down with the family, the hotel staff and customers in no time at all. The only problem was that Jake, after a few months of the 'high life', was getting a little overweight. So we suggested to Ron that it would be a good idea to cut out his breakfast in the morning. This message was duly passed on to the cook who prepared Jake's morning 'starter', which was, believe it or not, scrambled eggs, bacon and toast. Well, the thought of Jake not having his breakfast almost brought the kitchen to an industrial strike! If Jake could not have breakfast, then no-one was going to have breakfast. Hastily Ron reinstated Jake's meal and all was back to normal.

Jake has made many friends and admirers over the last few years and has attended all kind of events from banquets to pig roasts; he is also the best kind of 'security guard' when his master goes to the bank. All in all he is what a Rottweiler is all about: time and maturity has made him a natural guardian of his master's house, but most of all he is a much-loved member of a happy family. However, if he had not had such a sound temperament in his background breeding his harsh earlier experiences could have led to a very different story of Jake.

*   *   *

Operational guard dogs

Operational dogs have been known to cause embarrassment to their handlers. The present Guard Dogs Act 1975 was passed by Parliament because of unsatisfactory situations where unattended guard dogs savaged children who did not realise the dangers of trespassing on industrial property.

The headlines of a Sunday newspaper highlighted the fact that a police dog 'attacked' a linesman at a premier football match. The handler and dog were patrolling a very narrow strip between the bye-line and a low wall which separated the pitch from the terracing. The combination of the excited atmosphere from the crowd and the running linesman who suddenly raised his flag to denote an infringement as he passed the dog, was sufficient to trigger off a natural reaction. Police dogs no longer patrol that narrow strip of ground at this particular football ground.

'Excellent guard dogs on offer'

Most local newspapers feature a PETS FOR SALE or similar column, and one can usually find therein an insert offering a guard dog for sale. These advertisements normally follow a pattern and so do the reasons for selling; however, it is up to the buyer to discover the true reason for disposing of such a 'wonderful' guard dog. All too often a vice is being advertised as a virtue. The following are a selection of advertisements taken from a variety of local newspapers:

> JACK RUSSELL TERRIER – dog – 9 months old, excellent guard dog, not suitable for anyone with children.
>
> BORDER COLLIE – 10 months – Class 4 obedience, also excellent guard dog.
>
> DOBERMANN – bitch – 14 months old, excellent guard dog, temperament and pedigree, reared with children.
>
> GERMAN SHEPHERD DOG – 10 months old, Sire Breed Champion, excellent guard dog.
>
> DOBERMANN – dog – 8 months old, excellent guard dog, not accustomed to children.
>
> ALSATIAN – dog – 12 months – Sire Working Police Dog, intelligent, suitable for guarding duties.

Each of these dogs for sale has its own story to tell. Without seeing the dogs one can only assume that their present owners were duped into purchasing dogs completely unsuitable for a domestic environment. Occasionally such dogs are offered free to a good home, but the eventual cost may be substantial because of the liabilities which have been taken on unwittingly.

A study of these examples, which are typical, show certain patterns. Every one is an 'excellent guard dog', or potentially so, and they are generally youngsters. However, not one is advertised as a *trained* guard dog. Most of these dogs are too young to be trained as guards so it would appear that they are just noisy house dogs which are out of control. They have either been encouraged to bark or snarl, or they have been left to their own devices – but it is almost certain that the owners can no longer control the dogs and wish to pass on their failures and liabilities to someone else.

Other items within these advertisements can also give clues to possible problems. The Jack Russell (nine months), still a puppy and not suitable with children . . . I wonder why? Children are drawn to small dogs and what kind of home can this little dog go into with the certainty that it will never meet a child? It may, of course, guard the home *against* children. The fourteen-month-old Dobermann obviously adores children, but possibly to the extent that she is too ready to protect and defend them; she may even be uncontrollable because of it. The other Dobermann is not accustomed to children; this is possibly a cover for the dog's dislike of children. The owner of the German Shepherd probably paid a tidy sum for his highly pedigreed puppy and is using the Champion sire as an additional carrot to obtain a good price for a dog which is too young to be introduced to guarding duties by a pet dog owner. The Alsatian (which is a German Shepherd) has a sire which is a Working Police Dog. This is possible but unlikely. Police dogs are seldom used at stud and when they are the puppies are normally brought up as replacements for older dogs. Rejects may, of course, go into private homes. In this instance it would appear that the seller is hoping that someone will think that they are buying a police dog's offspring but I wonder why the dog is for sale? The Border Collie has obviously been taken to training classes and has reached Class 4, whatever that means. However, it is well known that dogs can work well in the obedience ring but outside it some owners haven't a clue as to how to control their dog's protective instincts. This may be a good buy, but . . .

In general, it is best to beware of advertisements which quote guarding qualities as a virtue. Remember that excellent and safe guard dogs require good control training which is effective at all times.

There are other ways of disposing of failures, but these are generally restricted to the popular working breeds. Security companies, Her Majesty's Forces or the police are happy to accept dogs which other people cannot handle. However, they all recognise that most of the dogs which are offered are considered by their owners to be a problem. A very high proportion of dogs on offer are rejected as unsuitable – the problem the domestic dog owner has is likely to cause the accepting authority the same difficulties. The problem may have to be trained out of the dog before constructive training can commence. It must also be remembered that police dogs normally live at the home of the handler as a member of the family while also being expected to do a job of work.

I recall one police dog handler whose old dog was due for retirement and he was looking at 'gift' dogs for a replacement. All the dogs on offer were German Shepherds and between one and two years of age. The first dog was very nervous and would require much work and time to counter his problem, with little guarantee of success. The second dog appeared to have been brought up in a negative environment and at eighteen months of age he had no motivation for anything. Again, time plus expertise did not equate with success. Dog number three was a character and was taken home on approval. He seemed ideal and was settling in nicely with no problems. However, on the third day the handler's eleven-year-old daughter went past the dog, who was lying in a doorway, to hang up her coat. The dog turned and bit her severely on the thigh – another reject. A deeper enquiry brought out the fact that the owner had encouraged this young dog to guard and protect his property and that the dog had already bitten someone. Hence the reason for disposing of the dog; he was now a liability. Dog number four came from an elderly couple who could not cope with their young German Shepherd's joy of living. He had no vices but did exactly what he wanted, and the elderly owners could do nothing about it. He has now learned discipline and control and is a happy dog: he enjoys tracking, he enjoys jumping, he enjoys attacking training 'criminals' and will defend his handler at all times. The juvenile delinquent has turned into a contented working dog with a purpose in life.

REMEMBER: MISUSE A DOG AND HIS VIRTUES BECOME VICES

Gate signs

Dog warning signs are now very much in fashion and are generally well presented. The illustrations show a selection produced by Birdbrook for the domestic market and can be obtained to depict almost any breed of dog

Gate signs come in many forms but wording must be chosen with care. A selection of examples follows.

with standard sets of wordings to suit your requirements. Care, however, should be taken in deciding just what you wish to convey to an intending visitor, welcome or not.

The legal implications of the wording on a sign must be given full consideration. All signs will act as a deterrent. Even the friendly-looking retrievers with the WE LIVE HERE and PLEASE CLOSE THE GATE is letting intending intruders know that dogs are present, but this in no way implies a risk to a legitimate visitor.

The Boxer with CAUTION – DOGS RUNNING FREE and DO NOT ENTER is positive with its instruction but leaves the word CAUTION, which has a variety of meanings in the dictionary, open to the individual's interpretation, but this may not relieve the owner of complete legal liability. A dog bite is never taken lightly in court and the defence of such a canine action may be difficult.

The Pug with CAUTION – I LIVE HERE can well be a notice to expect a dog when one enters. Some people have an unnatural fear of dogs and this

warning can be in their interest to ensure that they are not taken by surprise.

The Bull Terrier or Border Collie with the wording DOG ON DUTY makes it perfectly clear that anybody who is foolish enough to enter is likely to be attacked. However, the world is full of foolish people who require to be protected from their own actions. A junior who enters to retrieve his football can pay a heavy price for his escapade and the dog owner will not obtain immunity because of a sign fixed to the gate. However, a non-dog owner will have some peace of mind with such a sign fixed to his gate. Many a farmer has kept people off his land by displaying a sign with BEWARE OF THE BULL with not a bull in sight!

The Rottweiler and Dobermann with I AM ON GUARD HERE – ENTER ON YOUR OWN RESPONSIBILITY is a bold and meaningful sign. To use such a sign will certainly act as a strong deterrent but such a warning will not absolve the owner of his responsibilities.

The gate signs illustrated can be of great value but the use of a warning notice must not be allowed to overshadow a dog owner's moral and legal responsibility.

4 Legal Responsibilities

Introduction

All dog owners should appreciate their legal responsibilities, particularly when warning, guarding or protection duties are expected from their dogs. Just as people who threaten or act aggressively must consider the legal rights of others, it must be recognised that dogs are just an extension of their owners' actions and should be considered accordingly.

The law is a rather complicated subject and it is not expected that dog owners will understand the full legal implications of every canine action but I believe that a general background knowledge plus a sensible moral outlook should be sufficient to maintain an even balance of canine control.

A very good little book has been published to help dog owners understand their responsibilities and I would advise a study of this publication. The book is: *Your Dog and the Law* by Godfrey Sandys-Winsch (B.A.Cantab.), published by Shaw & Sons Ltd, 1984.

The domestic scene

The principal liability for the pet dog owner who regards his canine companion as a deterrent, can result from complaints that he owns a dangerous or ferocious dog. But what constitutes a dangerous or ferocious dog?

The Dogs Acts of 1871 and 1906 cover dangerous dogs although the 1906 Act seems to be confined to attacks on farm animals and horses. The 1871 Act seems to be more general but Section 2 states that a dog is normally classed as dangerous when it has attacked a person. It is also clear that it is not an offence to keep a dangerous dog but obviously if a dog has attacked someone and has been classed as dangerous and is still not being kept under proper control, a court order to keep the dog under control or have it destroyed could result. Any failure to comply with either order will make the owner liable to a penalty of £1 per day.

The fact that the dog happens to be on the owner's residential property when an attack takes place is unlikely to alter the situation if people have a right of access – and it can be very difficult to determine that people do *not* have a right of access. There are many more innocent people bitten when visiting a residential dwelling than those with criminal intent. In the latter case, one must determine the nature of criminal intent in relation to an attack and possible savaging from a dog. A schoolboy plundering an inviting apple tree certainly does not warrant being bitten or savaged by a dog, and this is likely to be the attitude of any sitting magistrate.

Although the legal definition of a ferocious dog does not appear to have been given specific interpretation, the meaning implies a dog with vicious tendencies. Any court will consider the behaviour of the dog at the time of the incident as well as any evidence of previous behaviour before passing judgment.

The only legal explanation I have found is given under Section 28 of the Town Police Clauses Act, 1847, where Item 80–1 states that it is an offence for 'Every person who suffers to be at large any unmuzzled ferocious dog, or sets on or urges any dog or other animal to attack, worry or put in fear any person or animal.'

It would appear that the meaning of this Act is restricted to public places and does not extend to the dog's behaviour on his own premises, be it residential or industrial. However, a dog which acts in a ferocious manner on private property is likely to take the first opportunity to bite a visitor and this possibility must always be a matter for serious consideration.

The operational scene

Although the legal implications of owning dangerous and ferocious dogs are discussed under the heading for the domestic scene they are equally applicable to dogs on operational duty. The same laws apply to the operational police dog, security-guard dogs or dogs which come under any other category.

However, the operational dog is more likely to be placed in a position where he will show his aggressive abilities through protective activities and, if misused or allowed to get out of control, the dog may then be classed as dangerous or ferocious. It will, therefore, be appreciated that dogs must be used with care when applied to operational situations.

The act of detaining a person is a matter which requires much consideration and this appears to come under the legal heading of 'powers of arrest'. There seem to be two general situations where persons other than police have the power to arrest another party and they are:

1. Power at common law (in respect of breach of the peace).
Any person may arrest where

(a) A breach of the peace is committed in the presence of the person making the arrest or

(b) The arrestor reasonably believes that such a breach will be committed in the immediate future by the arrested person although he has not yet committed any breach.

(c) Where a breach of the peace has been committed and it is reasonably believed that a renewal of it is threatened.

What exactly constitutes a breach of the peace is quite another matter but a physical attack or intended attack by an intruder on a householder, security guard or gamekeeper would appear to come under this category.

2. Power under the Criminal Law Act 1967 (Arrestable Offence). Under Section 2 (2) of the above Act 'Any person may arrest without warrant anyone who is or whom he, with reasonable cause, suspects to be in the act of committing an arrestable offence.

To apply this Act one must be clear on its definition. An arrestable offence is:

(a) one where sentence is fixed by law (e.g. murder – life imprisonment);
(b) one which is punishable by five years' imprisonment on first conviction or where the relevant statute says that it will be an arrestable offence (e.g. theft is punishable by ten years' imprisonment. All the offences involving a theft, such as burglary or robbery, come into this category);
(c) any attempt to commit (a) or (b).

Although these Acts go further than the brief details given, this information should give a handler some idea of his limitations.

The act of detaining a person is likely to involve the use of, or the threat to use, force. A dog's presence in certain circumstances may well be taken as a threat to apply force. The Criminal Law Act does give guidance on the use of force in effecting an arrest when applying the Common Law and Arrestable Offence powers. The Criminal Law Act 1967 Section 3 (1) states that 'A person may use such force as is reasonable in the circumstances in the prevention of crime, or in effecting or assisting in the lawful arrest of offenders or suspected offenders.'

If a handler uses his dog to effect an arrest the dog's actions are just an extension of those of the handler, and if the dog is used excessively or is allowed to go out of the handler's control then the handler must accept full responsibility for the injuries inflicted on the person being detained.

Dogs which are classed or used as guard dogs outside the application of a domestic situation are covered by the Guard Dogs Act 1975 which legislates for control and kennelling of such dogs. The Act is reproduced on the following pages in full:

Guard Dogs Act 1975

1975 CHAPTER 50

An Act to regulate the keeping and use of guard dogs; and for purposes connected therewith.

[1st August 1975]

BE IT ENACTED by the Queen's most Excellent Majesty, by and with the advice and consent of the Lords Spiritual and Temporal, and Commons, in this present Parliament assembled, and by the authority of the same, as follows:

Control of guard dogs

1.–(1) A person shall not use or permit the use of a guard dog at any premises unless a person ('the handler') who is capable of controlling the dog is present on the premises and the dog is under the control of the handler at all times while it is being so used except while it is secured so that it is not at liberty to go freely about the premises.

(2) The handler of a guard dog shall keep the dog under his control at all times while it is being used as a guard dog at any premises except–
   (*a*) while another handler has control over the dog; or
   (*b*) while the dog is secured so that it is not at liberty to go freely about the premises.

(3) A person shall not use or permit the use of a guard dog at any premises unless a notice containing a warning that a guard dog is present is clearly exhibited at each entrance to the premises.

Restriction of keeping guard dogs without a licence

2.–(1) A person shall not keep a dog at guard dog kennels unless he holds a licence under section 3 of this Act in respect of the kennels.

(2) A person shall not use or permit the use at any premises of a guard dog if he knows or has reasonable cause to suspect that the dog (when not being used as a guard dog) is normally kept at guard dog kennels in breach of subsection (1) of this section.

Guard dog kennel licences

3.–(1) A local authority may on the application in the prescribed form of, and on payment of the prescribed fee by, a person who runs or intends to run guard dog kennels at premises within their area grant that person a licence in respect of those kennels.

(2) A licence under this section shall be made subject to the prescribed conditions (if any) and to such other conditions as the local authority thinks fit.

(3) A licence under this section shall, subject to regulations, come into force on a date specified in the licence as the commencement date and shall expire at the end of the period of twelve months beginning with that date unless it is cancelled by a court in pursuance of the following subsection.

(4) Where a person is convicted of an offence under this Act, the Protection of Animals Act 1911, the Protection of Animals (Scotland) Act 1912, the Pet Animals Act 1951, the Animal Boarding Establishments Act 1963 or the Breeding of Dogs Act 1973, the court by which he is convicted may cancel any licence held by him under this Act.

1911 c. 27
1912 c. 14
1951 c. 35
1963 c. 43
1973 c. 60.

(5) The court may suspend the operation of the cancellation pending an appeal.

(6) For the purposes of this Act the Inner and Middle Temples shall be deemed to be in the City of London.

4.–(1) The applicant or, as the case may be, the licence holder may appeal to a magistrates' court or, in Scotland, a sheriff court, against–

Appeals

- (*a*) the refusal of a local authority to grant a licence; or
- (*b*) the conditions (other than the prescribed conditions) to which the licence is subject; or
- (*c*) the authority's refusal to vary the conditions; or
- (*d*) the revocation of a licence.

(2) On an appeal the court may, if it thinks fit, give directions to the local authority with respect to the licence or the conditions, and it shall be the duty of the local authority to comply with such directions.

5.–(1) A person who contravenes section 1 or 2 of this Act shall be guilty of an offence and liable on summary conviction to a fine not exceeding £400.

Offences, penalties and civil liability

(2) The provisions of this Act shall not be construed as–
- (*a*) conferring a right of action in any civil proceedings (other than proceedings for the recovery of a fine or any prescribed fee) in respect of any contravention of this Act or of any regulations made under this Act or of any of the terms or conditions of a licence granted under section 3 of this Act; or
- (*b*) derogating from any right of action or other remedy (whether civil or criminal) in proceedings instituted otherwise than by virtue of this Act.

6.–(1) Regulations may be made–

Regulations

- (*a*) enabling a local authority to revoke a licence and, on the application of the licence holder, to vary the conditions (other than the prescribed conditions) of the licence;
- (*b*) requiring the payment of the prescribed fee to be made to a local authority on inspection by the authority of premises in respect of which an application for a licence has been made;
- (*c*) providing for the continuance or transfer of the licence where an appeal is made, and on the death of the licence holder.

(2) Any power to make regulations under this Act–

(*a*) may be exercised so as to make different provisions for different cases or different classes of cases;

(*b*) includes power to make such incidental or supplemental provision in the regulations as the Secretary of State considers appropriate.

(3) Regulations under this Act shall be made by statutory instrument which shall be subject to annulment by resolution of either House of Parliament.

Interpretation

1953 c. 28

7. In this Act, unless the context otherwise requires–

'agricultural land' has the same meaning as in the Dogs (Protection of Livestock) Act 1953;

'guard dog' means a dog which is being used to protect–

(*a*) premises; or

(*b*) property kept on the premises; or

(*c*) a person guarding the premises or such property;

'guard dog kennels' means a place where a person in the course of business keeps a dog which (notwithstanding that it is used for other purposes) is used as a guard dog elsewhere, other than a dog which is used as a guard dog only at premises belonging to its owner;

'local authority' means, in relation to England and Wales, a district council, a London borough council and the Common Council of the City of London, and, in relation to Scotland, an islands council or a district council;

'premises' means land other than agricultural land and land within the curtilage of a dwelling-house, and buildings, including parts of buildings, other than dwelling-houses;

'prescribed' means prescribed by regulations;

'regulations' means regulations made by the Secretary of State.

Short title, commencement and extent

8.–(1) This Act may be cited as the Guard Dogs Act 1975.

(2) This Act shall come into force on such day as the Secretary of State may by order made by statutory instrument appoint, and different days may be so appointed for, or for different purposes of, different provisions.

(3) This Act does not extend to Northern Ireland.

5 Control Training

Introduction

Control training is the most important feature of a training programme which involves any of the guarding features already discussed.

To have a dog walk under perfect but not obvious control by his handler's side during a stressful situation is essential. The dog which shows aggressive tendencies to the extent that the handler is preoccupied in controlling the dog whilst trying to communicate with another person, can prevent that handler from giving due attention to the situation at hand.

The dog which does not stay on command, either when at the handler's side or whilst away from him, will again be uncontrollable when the need is greatest.

The dog which does not come back when called whilst under normal conditions can never be considered to be reliable or controllable and is quite unsuited to any of the guarding functions.

Because a dog does not meet any of the basic control requirements, or is even impossible to handle, does not mean to say that he cannot be trained to become a suitable candidate for guarding duties. Such a dog may well be limited in the duties he can perform but these limitations are more likely to be governed by the abilities and character of the trainer or the eventual handler.

The dog pictured on the cover of this book with his Park Security handler was such an animal. This German Shepherd named Sabre was of good sound breeding but was completely unmanageable. Sabre was brought up in a domestic environment where the dog's natural protective instincts were permitted to take over and, for all we know, the protectiveness may have been encouraged at an early and impressionable age.

At the age of about twelve months the situation became so serious that the dog was to have been put down if a suitable alternative could not be found. A change to another domestic environment was considered to be out of the question.

Sabre went to Callanway Dog Training establishment as a last resort to see if there was any possibility of giving him a future. Initially he proved to be quite unmanageable and aggressive with everybody. However, each such dog must finally come round to accepting someone as a friend. After

Sabre can accept an innocent child (ABOVE) but will attack as necessary. (BELOW)

a couple of weeks in the kennels, Eric Roberts, the proprietor and chief trainer, became that friend. A constructive assessment was sufficient to show Sabre's true character and his ability to act with responsibility. There was, after all, a place in this world for Sabre, even after such a bad beginning.

Eric could see the potential in this dog and so could Ian Griffiths, the Country Park Security Officer, who took Sabre and trained him to be his working companion and protector.

The photographs of Sabre show that he is now equally at home with an enquiring child as he is with a trouble-making adult whilst he is on duty in his country park.

Basic principles

To carry out any form of dog training, be it a simple control exercise or the more demanding requirements for any of the guarding duties, it is essential to appreciate the most basic of training principles.

It should be recognised that dogs learn something every day. They can learn by accident or by design. Learning by accident is when things just happen; they may be unconsciously created by the handler. Just being alive will create learning experiences. Learning by design takes place with constructive training or when situations are set up to create specific experiences.

Although learning by accident cannot be completely avoided, an appreciation of the fact can help handlers to minimise the experiences which would have an adverse effect on the dog's future. Learning by design does not need to be restricted to planned sessions of training but it should become a way of life.

The art of communication

Visual or verbal instructions to a dog must be understood before they can be obeyed. To understand them, a dog must be able to translate his handler's instructions into something which makes sense to him. This means that we start off with a language barrier and so throughout the training cycle with a dog this barrier must be broken down.

To tell a dog to sit-stay or come to you is quite useless if he does not understand the meaning of these instructions; neither will he learn the meaning unless he can associate the words with particular requirements. It can therefore be said that dogs learn from actions and the understanding of words comes later, although in some instances it may not be much later.

Sign language and physical assistance are very important aspects of dog training, especially in the earlier stages of any instruction being taught. Every movement or utterance tells a dog something, but he will only

Hands and voice maintain Corrie's attention.

respond satisfactorily to a handler's wishes if he feels that the instruction is of value to him. A dog will apply canine logic to every request which is made of him. The nature of the instruction and the manner in which it is given will have an effect on his response.

Using a nice quiet voice when instructing a dog to come to you may well have the desired reaction if the dog has nothing better to do. However, to carry out the same procedure and in the same tone of voice whilst the dog has an interesting distraction is likely to be met with a deaf ear. In this instance, sharpness in the voice will probably be required to gain his attention and the gentle instruction can then have the desired effect. A dog will always react in a manner which he thinks is in his best interest. That is canine logic and it is often far removed from our own understanding of human logic.

This situation often results in a conflict of interests – owner interest against that of his dog. It may well be in the owner's interest that a dog barks to give warning of a stranger approaching his home. However, it is also in the owner's interest that the barking stops when he is satisfied that sufficient warning has been given. That single act of barking is initially in the interest of both owner and dog. As soon as the owner is satisfied that the stranger is welcome, the owner's requirements change: warning has been given and the dog's barking now becomes a nuisance. However, to the dog, the situation may not have altered and he may feel that he should keep on barking. The owner must convince his dog that the objective has been achieved without devaluing the dog's guarding function because on future occasions the dog will be required to give warning of approaching strangers.

Basic equipment

The basic equipment to assist with control training can simply be listed as:
 (1) collar
 (2) lead
 (3) possibly a long line
The choice of collar and lead can play a significant part in a handler's ability to control and train his dog.

Collars
A collar of the type which tightens and checks a dog's activities is advisable and all basic training should be carried out using one.

A metal-link *check* or *choke* chain is the most common type of collar available and, when correctly used, can be very effective. A good quality leather or nylon rope collar which acts on the same principle will not cut into the hairs round a dog's neck as will the metal-link type collar.

The *Combi-collar* is another useful and effective collar and is usually made of webbing, nylon or cotton, with a chain loop which creates a tightening round the dog's neck. This type of collar can be adjusted and, with its limited tightening effect, will not choke the dog.

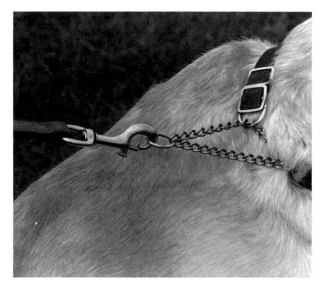

A combi-collar – also a strong trigger clip on lead.

Correct fitting of check chain, but demonstrated on left wrist.

Incorrect fitting of check chain, will not slacken when released.

Leads

A good strong lead of suitable length is an essential piece of equipment. The standard length of four to five feet is quite satisfactory although the police type of double lead can have its advantages during the more advanced training.

The lead must have strength. A good quality leather lead which has been well softened with a well-known leather dressing is well worth having and a pleasure to handle. A good quality nylon or cotton webbing lead can be quite satisfactory and is a reasonably priced substitute for leather.

The strength of a lead may well depend on the clip and its attachment. A lead should always be examined in detail before purchase to ensure that it will stand up to the hard work which will be demanded of it. The trigger style of clip is probably the most suitable as it incorporates strength and safety and is easy to release when required.

Police-style lead with
trigger clip at each end
and suitably placed rings
to create varying lengths.

A long line

This is principally for the dog which is likely to play up when out of the
handler's immediate control. A line of some thirty to forty feet in length
will probably be satisfactory. A nylon cord with a breaking strain of 700 lb
or over should suit most dogs and can be purchased from hardware or
sports shops.

A trigger-style dog-lead clip should be tied to one end with a holding
loop at the other.

All-in-one leather lead
and collar; the silent
application is ideal for
night work.

Control exercises

The basic control exercises which must be considered as essential requirements for the foundation of any guarding duties are:
(1) to come back when called;
(2) to walk at heel on a loose lead and also without a lead; and
(3) to stay in the stand, sit or down positions at distances within the requirements of the particular guarding or protection function.
This control should initially be attained under conditions which are
relatively free from stress or distractions but eventually it will be achieved
in more demanding situations.

Getting and keeping your dog's attention is the name of the game.
Without that ability you are lost. Every training action or element is based
on the premise that you can call your dog's name and receive his *immediate*
attention.

Attentiveness is the answer and should be based on canine interest.
Without his interest you cannot get his attention and unless you have his
attention he will go his own way.

Gaining your dog's attention
This is the initial requirement for every exercise and is to be maintained as
a principal requirement at any time during the dog's guarding life. It
should, of course, be of prime importance to any dog owner.

Your dog's response to the call of his name is the key to obtaining his

Corrie's handler moves to
tap his hindquarters to
obtain an immediate
response.

attention. A tap or slap on the hindquarters, if he is close enough, as you call his name may well be sufficient. A short sharp tug of the lead or long line can be part of the attention-getting routine. Each action which gains his attention should coincide with the use of his name.

His name must be used in a manner which suits the situation: your tone may be gentle and encouraging, or it may be firm with strength. Avoid asking for your dog's attention when you expect failure; rather deploy yourself where success is guaranteed.

Initial training can be carried out on the lead or a long line where your dog has a certain amount of freedom to investigate interesting smells at varying distances from you. When you are ready give a tug on the lead or line with just sufficient force to gain his attention as you call his name.

Each time you call for your dog's attention and get it, follow up your reason for requiring his attention and then give him his reward. Your dog will soon realise that it is worth his while to give you his attention. Fun with a toy or titbits of food, along with praise and affection, are the ingredients for an appreciated reward.

To come back when called

There are times when you can make use of natural opportunities to call your dog back with guaranteed success. You should also practise the recall at proper training sessions to ensure that your dog understands the meaning of your requirements.

As a trainer you must learn to take advantage of your dog's natural responses to everyday situations: e.g. at feeding times when he hears his food being made up, or when it is time for a walk and the picking up of his lead is enough to let him know he is going out. A second before you make your intentions known to your dog, call his name and add the instruction to come. The noise of his feeding dish or the picking up of the lead will create the response and thereby give meaning to the instruction.

Individual and prepared training sessions can provide the more demanding aspect for an obedient response where the principal reward may eventually be words of praise and a gentle but appreciative stroke of the head.

Build up on a background of success and take any failure as an indication of your own (not the dog's) deficiency in assessing the situation or applying the procedure.

The principal causes of failure can be split into two categories:

(a) *Strength of distraction.*

A dog will usually come back to his owner when there is no good reason for staying away. An interesting smell, an amorous bitch, a playful canine companion or fear of his own master are all good canine reasons for not answering the call to come back.

(b) *Distance between dog and handler*.

This combined with the strength of a distraction can be a very powerful factor. When a dog is only one pace away from his handler he will be much more responsive than if he is at a distance of thirty paces. The greater the distance the more defiant he can become, unless he is the type of dog which has a sense of insecurity at a distance. With the latter situation, it can be an advantage to create distance between the inattentive but insecure dog and his handler.

During all recall training or guarding situations the foregoing factors must be recognised, with the approach to handling being continually adjusted in order to achieve success.

With success in gaining your dog's attention under your belt it may be that a domestic standard of recall comes naturally to your dog and without a great deal of effort on your part. However, for the dog which is expected to receive training in the field of guarding duties then a more purposeful and demanding approach is a *necessity*.

Basic recall training is best carried out on the lead and can be combined with the first stage of loose lead walking. This is really a follow-on from the attention-getting exercise, whereby you keep your dog's mind attentively on you in a manner which will ensure that he will move in the same direction as yourself and as close as is practicable. Make use of a slip collar or combi-collar and a good lead of suitable length. Remember that a short lead will reduce the effect of your training approach.

Initially, you should endeavour to work with the minimum of distractions. With your dog on the lead start by giving him a minute or so to sniff around and become bored with the lack of activity on your part. When he has found a distraction or is just plain bored, create a positive action at your end of the lead. Move away and backwards smartly, call your dog's name and instruct him to come with you. If necessary give a purposeful tug on the lead, but also give plenty of enthusiasm, encouragement and praise.

On some occasions stop to give the dog praise and on others change direction to move forward so that he can be encouraged to fall in at your left side. Five to ten paces at your side should initially be quite sufficient. Always finish with praise and a game or titbit.

Build up on this procedure with distractions of varying degrees; this will give the foundation for a very attentive dog who is ready to come back immediately he is called.

Testing to assess your progress can be done by replacing the lead with a long line. The degree of your success will be revealed when you let your dog drag the line and then call him to you when he is interested in some minor distraction. A satisfactory response can lead on to the involvement of stronger distractions while still using the long line in place of the lead.

Any failure to respond immediately to your instruction must be

Hand and body actions
help to achieve a
responsive recall.

countered by strength of purpose. Take the end of the line and treat it like
the lead (as already described) for gaining your dog's attention. Ensure a
reliable response for a period on the line before attempting a completely
free situation with distractions.

Remember the importance of achieving success time and time again at
close range before attempting to build up on distances.

Loose lead walking
The ultimate objective of this training exercise is to have your dog walking
at your left side conscious of and responsive to your every movement. Thus
the early stages of recall training on the lead represent the groundwork for
loose lead walking.

At this stage loose lead walking can begin from a free on-lead situation
and finish in a like manner. To make a dog sit at the start or finish *at this
stage* could have an inhibiting effect: it is important to have a keen and
attentive dog. Basic sit training should be accomplished in a prompt and
satisfactory manner quite independent of loose lead walking. When a
sound foundation of walking at heel on a loose lead has been achieved the
sit can be incorporated at the start and finish of the training routine.

It should be noted that there may well be occasions in the future when
you will be pleased to have your dog pull you at the end of the lead, particularly during the training for protection work, and this must be kept ᴉ mind
whilst teaching a dog to walk on a loose lead. There will, then, be occasions
when you allow your dog to pull and it is important that he knows you are
permitting such an action. If your loose lead walking is strict, with no
opportunity to pull, then problems can be created during advanced

training. When you do permit your dog to pull on the lead, encourage him positively so that he fully understands the difference in your requirements.

Back to loose lead walking and making your dog conscious of your every movement. When your dog is fully responsive to your backward and forward movements with him on a loose lead, the forward movement can become the principal direction bearing in mind that any inattention or distraction can instantly be countered by a quick change to a backward movement in order to regain his attention.

The approach with each particular dog must be varied to suit his normal attitude to loose lead walking. The dog which plods along is unlikely to be more than just a warning dog and may not be required to walk attentively at heel, but if this *is* a requirement then handler enthusiasm and great encouragement are required during loose lead walking.

The keen energetic dog which is more likely to be a real guarding prospect, will probably require to be taken in hand. He is likely to be the kind which forges ahead and this could be difficult to control when guarding or protective instincts come to the fore.

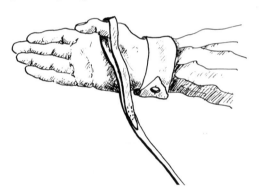

First stage in lead holding during training.

The hold on and use of the lead are important factors in correct loose lead walking. Although the end of the lead is held in the right hand it is the left hand which does most of the work. Give your dog as little lead as possible but never with tension. The exception to this is in giving a jerk back, when you do so with a quick check and release action.

The left hand can be used as a guide for the lead to slip through, it can be used to hold the lead when required and it can also be taken from the lead and used for visual encouragement.

Your dog should respond to your actions and verbal encouragement with commands, as such, being unnecessary. An appropriate phrase or sentence can be used in a manner suited to the circumstances. The word '*Heel*' within the phrase is probably most apt with 'Come on, son, *heel*, that's a good boy,' as good a line as any.

Your forward movement should initially be devoid of sharp turns. A single straight line, or walking in a circle with the dog on the inside, are two

Holding lead correctly in right hand with left hand ready for action as required.

good approaches. To start with, the circle can be some 20 feet plus in diameter, but as proficiency is attained this can be brought down to a diameter of some 15 feet for short spells of work.

The large circle will avoid the need for sharp turns until loose lead walking is achieved with dedicated canine attention for some twenty to thirty seconds of continuous work.

By this time an obedient sit when instructed should be attained through a separate training routine and this exercise can now be added to the loose lead walking routine. A prompt sit before starting will ensure the dog's attention and should not lead to any problems. However, a smart halt with a prompt sit during or on completion of a training routine will require training and will probably take you back to the earliest stage of sit training, i.e. where you take the lead in your right hand as near as possible to the collar and at the same time push with the left hand in and down at the left side of the dog's croup. This will ensure an instant response. Praise should always follow the completion of the routine (or any part of it) when the display of your satisfaction will help to maintain a pleasant relationship.

The introduction of sharp left and right turns can now be introduced to help attain and to assess the attentiveness of your dog. When inattention results in a poorly executed turn a quick backward movement can replace the turn to keep the dog on his toes and fully alert.

Off-lead situations can now be introduced for very short spells so that you can measure the degree of your success. This, along with other basic training routines, can create the control required for more stressful situations when guarding and protection training requires absolute control.

The stay exercises

Control in achieving a static canine position is an essential ingredient within a basic training programme. To stay in the sit, down and stand positions is certainly desirable, but all three may not be essential for a guard or protection dog.

The sit position is ideal for short-term control and can be used during many everyday situations. It is also an intermediate stage in teaching your dog to go down and stay in that position.

Down and stay training is much more demanding and can be used within two principal concepts: (a) a long and relaxed down whilst the handler is free to carry out some other function, and this may well be out of the dog's sight; (b) in an aggressive situation where the handler is required to deal with the problem. In this latter instance the dog would be put into the down position at the handler's side and expected to stay there whilst, say, a heated discussion takes place. This can be a rather difficult time for a dog when he feels that he should be in there giving physical support to a verbal situation, hence the need for a sound basic training procedure.

The stand and stay position has great value when neither the sit nor down are practical or realistic. It is often easier to ask a dog to stay where he is standing and possibly ready to move, or to stop him on the move without the excessive demand to go down or to come back.

A guarding dog is likely to move towards any unknown visitor in a manner which can be rather menacing; to ask him to come back may put doubt in the dog's mind at the moment when the handler requires a continuation of the guarding role. To ask him to sit or go down may well be beyond his training for the situation in hand. However, to demand a stay whilst he maintains an attentive attitude can give the handler time to reach the dog and control the situation without upsetting any of the animal's guarding instincts or his response to further training.

Now to the training procedures for the various stay positions. Stand and sit training can be carried out during the same period with the down following the initial stages of sit training.

STAND-STAY It should not be considered necessary at any time during this training routine to purposely put the dog into the stand position. If the dog happens to be sitting or lying down then it is logical to carry on with the stay training in that position.

Stand-stay training is, therefore, best introduced when the dog is on the lead and on the move. It is also presumed that there are occasions when the dog is permitted to pull on the lead. It may in fact be advisable to create situations where the dog wants to move forward and ahead of you, for instance, to meet another member of the family.

On such occasions give a very firm instruction to stay and couple this with tension on the lead to halt him. After a few seconds release the tension a little. Any attempt from the dog to move forward must be stopped by a resumption of lead tension and the repeated instruction to stay. Continue to ease off the lead tension and repeat the instruction until your dog is prepared to stay. At that moment give some gentle praise but not sufficient to distract him from his reason for wanting to move forward.

The praise may well give your dog the impression that he is being permitted to move forward. If this happens repeat the exercise with the lead tension and the instruction to stay. Continue with the praise and lead tension routine until your dog is prepared to remain standing on the one spot on a loose lead as you give him enthusiastic praise. However, this procedure should still be carried out without taking his attention from his reason for wanting to move forward.

Build up to ten or fifteen seconds before giving permission to break from the stand and stay position. When your dog is prepared to stop and stand when instructed without any tension on the lead it is likely that he is now ready to carry out a similar routine exercise whilst off the lead.

Whilst your dog is free but relatively close to you, up to three or four yards away, and moving with little to take his interest, give the prompt instruction to stay. Verbally keep him there, go to him, give him praise then release him from the position.

You should practise the exercise with him on the lead during more stressful situations, using the routine above. Success will be indicated by an immediate response to the stay instruction without requiring to use any tension on the lead.

Vary the situations for staying when instructed, and remember that special training periods can be less frequent if natural opportunities are taken during normal daily activities. Select some occasions when distractions are minimal, and at other times take advantage of stressful situations to consolidate on a prompt response to the stay instruction. Sometimes you can finish the exercise by calling your dog to you, at other times you can go to him; but always finish with praise.

Create versatility in your application of the stay at the stand as this is an excellent foundation for the control which will be so necessary during guarding operations.

SIT-STAY To obtain promptness in achieving a sit position it is preferable to have your dog on the lead during the early stages of training. With your dog at your left side whilst you are stationary, or on the move, take a very short

Physically assisting Blue
(Jaelr Royale C.D.Ex.)
into sit position.

Completing the assisted
sit.

grip on your lead with the right hand and as near to the collar as possible. At the same time put your left hand at the left side of your dog's croup, push his rear end down and towards you as your right hand pulls up on the lead. This double action must be properly co-ordinated and carried out with purpose.

As you start to carry out this double action use a gentle voice of encouragement, 'That's a good boy,' but as soon as he starts moving into the sit give a firm 'Sit!' instruction. On completion of the movement give your dog praise but ensure that he makes no attempt to move. In these early lessons a five-second compulsory sit is probably sufficient before giving the dog his freedom.

Your dog will soon anticipate and start moving into the sit position as soon as you go into the routine of taking the lead in the right hand and putting your left hand by the croup.

Do not move on to more progressive exercises until your dog responds to the sit instruction in a prompt and purposeful manner, and without any physical assistance from you.

Ensuring a contented and stable stay at the sit.

To ensure that your dog stays in the sitting position, stand straddled over him and facing in the same direction. By doing this you can prevent him from getting up or going down. This also allows you to stroke your dog's neck to give him reassurance, yet you can take your hands away but have them available to restrain him if he thinks of moving. During this period keep instructing your dog to stay.

To consolidate and make your intentions perfectly clear to your dog, create inducements which will entice him to move whilst you are in a position to control the situation. Give some gentle praise in a more enthusiastic manner; this will create stressful situations which can induce your dog to move. Whilst you are standing straddled over him you can prevent this movement and ensure that your dog knows the meaning of the instruction to stay. Do not move from the straddled position until your dog accepts enthusiastic praise without any attempt to move. By this time a solid foundation for progression will have been achieved.

The next stage is to walk round your dog, but still holding the lead and continuing with the instruction to stay. If you use your dog's name it is important not to do so at the start of a verbal instruction, or he may expect a recall. I tend to drop the dog's name completely when training for all the stay exercises. 'Sit and stay, son' or just 'Stay where you are, son' is quite sufficient. It is, of course, important to bring out the word *stay* with some strength, but not necessarily with volume. Remember that your dog's name is the attention-getter and is usually followed by a more active situation than staying in the one position.

Gradually build up on distance and time in the stay position, initially with the lead attached but eventually without the lead. Always go back to your dog otherwise he may anticipate a recall and start breaking from the stay situation.

Up to a minute at the sit-stay and at a distance of some 20 yards is quite sufficient for this exercise. Anything beyond those requirements would be more suited to a down and stay situation.

DOWN-STAY Again the down instruction must create an instant response; it is preferable not to start the down exercise until the early stages of the sit have been suitably covered. The down can then be more easily executed from the sit position. As the down is a very submissive action it is preferable to go down from a semi-submissive state (sit) rather than from a free standing position, certainly during the earlier stages of training.

Have your dog sitting at your left side and put yourself into a kneeling position. Put your left arm over the dog's shoulder so that your left hand is positioned behind his left pastern. Whilst doing this put your right hand behind his right pastern, then push his front feet forward so that he will drop onto his chest. At the same time let your own body weight drop so that

LEFT AND OPPOSITE The three movements from the sit to the down position.

you can rest with your left elbow on the ground if desired.

Firmness in your action followed by praise will soon let your dog know that an instant response is essential – you will accept nothing less. When your dog anticipates your action and starts to move into the down position just as you are preparing to give physical assistance, give the instruction to go down. As with the sit exercise earlier this can be in the form of a phrase – 'Down you go, son' – with emphasis on the 'down'.

You must be alert for any attempt by the dog to get up; such a move can be easily countered initially from your kneeling position. As with the stay at the sit, give gentle praise and then go on to praise in a more enthusiastic manner; this will soon again create a situation where your dog is likely to get up. However, as you are kneeling beside him you can prevent any such movement and at the same time ensure that your dog understands the meaning of the down-and-stay instruction. When your dog accepts enthusiastic praise without any attempt to move, then sufficient progress has been made to enable you to move a little distance from him.

Gradually build up on the distance and the time that you are away from your dog, but during this process continue to instruct him to stay and then follow up with praise, quite enthusiastically at times. Any indication of the dog's intention to move must be countered before he has reached the stage of changing position. The stay at the down without a hint of moving, whilst you continue to give enthusiastic praise, is the best indication of commitment on the part of your dog.

Your dog will soon learn the meaning of the command to go down from the sit when the verbal instructions are accompanied by the visual signal of your hand indicating the ground. Once the dog fully understands the verbal and visual instructions he will then respond to the same instructions from a natural standing situation. Whilst he is on the lead give the down instruction and bring your body down in a manner which gives a slight tug down on the collar in order to obtain your objective.

Remember the need for an *instant* response at all times. It should not be necessary to repeat the instruction once the dog understands what is required of him. At a later stage in training for advanced guarding or protection work the value of this ground work will become more apparent. An unreliable stayer will reveal a slip-shod approach in the earlier days of training.

When the build-up of time and distance has reached some five minutes of your absence and a distance of some 20 to 30 yards, it would be opportune to introduce some mild aggravation between yourself and a helpful assistant so that you can watch your dog's reaction and be ready to counter any thought of movement on his part.

Downing your dog at any time and at any distance is the final stage of this basic training routine. When you are out for a walk with your dog and he has freedom of movement whilst off the lead, give a firm instruction to go down at a moment when nothing seems to be on his mind. Start with a minimal distance between you and your dog, say less than 10 yards. First, call his name to get his immediate attention, then instruct him to go down. As the situation is quite new to him he may not go down at once. Walk towards him, keep him at the one spot then down him. He will soon understand the new development and greater distances can then be employed.

Advantage can also be taken of distractions. When your dog's mind is on

Shadowsquad Callum of
Ardfern C.D.Ex.
U.D.Ex. W.D.Ex.
P.D.Ex.

something other than yourself, give the instruction to go down, but you must first call his name as an attention-getter. If the distraction proves too much and he has not responded to your call go nearer to him and again demand his attention before giving the instruction to go down.

Unless complete control has been attained under normal and slightly stressful situations always go to your dog rather than break the stay from a distance; this will prevent anticipation on his part.

Although the sit-stay will certainly have its value, the training to stay at any distance or to go down and stay are essentials which cannot be neglected. Any failure to appreciate these requirements will certainly show up as a lack of control and may even result in legal action when a practical situation results in an unwarranted attack by your dog on some party.

6 Training for Guarding Duties

Introduction

Responsibilities must now be faced and an honest assessment is required before proceeding to the training routines for guard work. A dog well trained in guarding or protection duties, in the hands of a responsible owner, is as safe as any dog – in fact much safer than many a dog which has had no formal training of any kind. The latter, in the hands of an unsuitable owner, can be as dangerous as a badly trained dog. (I shall continue to emphasise how important is the need for the owner or handler to recognise his/her responsibilities when a dog is trained for guard work.)

I have experienced both the safe and the unreliable dogs, but fortunately have only lived with dogs which were perfectly safe. Two such dogs were my German Shepherds which qualified through the Police Dog Stake (P.D.) at working trials. W.T. Ch. Quest of Ardfern C.D.Ex., U.D.Ex., P.D.Ex., T.D.Ex., won his first two entries into the P.D. Stakes where a section of the work called for the stiffest requirements in guarding and protection work which included

(a) Quarter and search for a criminal, also indicating and maintaining contact.
(b) Test of courage – being threatened with a gun or stick, also aggressive noise from the criminal, such as banging a dustbin lid with a stick.
(c) Food refusal.
(d) Escorting a criminal and defending the handler during an unexpected attack.
(e) Pursuit of a criminal and forcibly detaining him.
(f) Being recalled whilst in full flight after a suspected person who is running away. This proves control and stability.

The other dog, Shadowsquad Callum of Ardfern, C.D.Ex., U.D.Ex., W.D.Ex., P.D.Ex., was placed second and qualified in his only entry into the P.D. Stake. Hip displasia terminated his career at that stage.

Both these dogs were excellent at their job, particularly Callum who had a reputation amongst training criminals of being a very hard dog. He was given two nicknames, the Bone Cruncher and Cree's Biting Machine. Yet both Callum and Quest lived as pets at home where there were my two young daughters and their friends about the place. These dogs were treated as members of the family and were completely trustworthy in all situations.

One unusual incident involving Callum brought forth a beautifully controlled reaction. We went out for his last exercise one dark Saturday evening and were walking across a piece of waste ground when I heard a noise. It was a youth, who was enjoying a rather stupid prank of kicking over the lamps round a trench in the road. I came out of the darkness with Callum by my side and challenged the youth with a few choice words for this stupid and dangerous piece of 'fun'. Our, or Callum's, presence persuaded the youth to return to the trench and fix the lamps. Although till now I had not been aware of Callum's demeanour I suddenly realised that he was performing a perfect escort of the 'criminal'. He reacted automatically to all his previous training, was fully alert because of my own attitude, and was ready to handle an attack on my person or an attempt to run away. Callum was already on the lead and I permitted him to carry out his 'escort duties'.

Before you embark on the training of your dog for guard work, you should be able to give satisfactory answers to the following questions:

(1) Is your dog a suitable candidate for the more advanced requirements of guarding and protection work? If so, how far along the road can he be taken with absolute safety?

(2) Do you have the strength of character, the patience and the ability to handle such a dog? What are your limitations?

(3) Do you have the assistance of a suitable experienced person to help you achieve your objective?

Any failure to match up with these very strict requirements can result in disaster. I recall, some years ago, an acquaintance who was a very successful obedience competitor. He had apparently been carrying out protection work training with a group of enthusiasts who were relatively inexperienced in the art of such training. I met up with this gentleman at some event and at the time was not aware that he was dabbling in protection work. I spotted him, his dog by his side, and greeted him with a friendly slap on the shoulder. The response from his dog was immediate and terrifying as the animal turned to attack me. Fortunately his handler had experienced this before and his reaction was equally quick, terminating the attack before the dog's jaws closed on my arm. A lucky day for me but for the owner a situation extremely difficult to live with. Since those early days this particular handler has owned a few other dogs and all have been completely trustworthy. The behaviour of that first dog did not match up to the absolute requirements of a guard dog. The situation was apparently due to the unsuitability of the training approach with the training 'criminal' being primarily responsible (see point no. 3 above).

The earlier chapters have dealt with some of the requirements from both dog and handler. The training 'criminal' is the next important ingredient to be added to the recipe.

The 'criminal' or intruder, as he will be called throughout this book, is the person who is the agitator for the dog, the person who hides from the dog. He is the real trainer, the person who brings out the dog's alertness, who helps to ensure that the dog indicates a presence and that he maintains an interest in that presence. The 'criminal' also plays a major role in ensuring that a dog bites properly during protection-work training.

Added to this, the 'criminal's' function is also to control the activities of the handler. The handler must always position himself and act as he is instructed, also apply the correct measure of control on his dog as and when the 'criminal' indicates.

Any one of the training activities which affect canine aggressive instincts requires the involvement of a good 'criminal'; he can make or break a dog. Anybody who is interested in entering the field of dog training for guard work should make sure they have engaged the services of a 'criminal' who can apply a sensible and trustworthy approach. There are plenty of people around who lay claim to such expertise, but it would be advisable to view the results of their efforts before allowing them to tamper with your dog. Remember, the end result is *your* responsibility and not that of the training 'criminal'.

Of course, with the training of a warning dog, where no aggressive reactions are required, a sensible approach by the owner with the help of family members or friends should achieve effective and safe results.

An awareness and indication of a presence

There is little value in having a dog become aware of somebody approaching, be it at home, on duty within a guarding environment or while out for a walk, if he does not give a suitable indication of that presence. That being the case, we combine the subjects of awareness and indication.

An alertness to somebody approaching is the most natural response for most dogs but a little help and encouragement may be required to let a dog know that his alertness is appreciated.

Although there should be sufficient opportunities in every-day life to observe a dog's reaction, special sessions can be added to simulate unusual occurrences at times when there is a particular need for an attentive canine outlook. It is the slamming of a car door, the opening of a gate, the footsteps on the path or the knock on the front door which should bring the domestic watch dog to life. The professional dog will be brought to life in a similar manner but the circumstances may be more in keeping with advanced guarding functions.

The dog which does not respond to external activity can be prompted by an urgent question – 'What was that, Ben?' or something similar. However, be it natural or assisted, immediate praise should be the reward for paying attention to the external activity. If assistance is required from outside, have a relative or friend make more noise than usual to draw attention to an external activity. Do not be satisfied until your dog is reacting immediately to movements that you are aware of. Remember that your dog can use ears, nose and the feeling of movement to inform him of a presence.

How he indicates a presence is the factor which is now of importance. You may be satisfied with an excited dog trying to gain your attention, or you may want him to bark. A barking dog will gain your attention and will also warn a visitor of his own presence. This will certainly make the unwanted visitor think twice about proceeding with any undesirable activities.

If you wish to have your dog speak (bark) as an indication of a presence, the full procedure for teaching such a response is given at this point and will be considered as a necessity for some of the more demanding guarding or protection requirements.

To speak when required

It should initially be recognised that some dogs may never be taught to speak (bark) when required, also that the conditions which prevent a dog doing so today can change and he can become an ideal pupil at some later date.

The desire to bark may have been so well suppressed in the past by the handler, or some other party, that the change may not be practicable. I have owned dogs which have been easy and others which have been very difficult, as well as dogs which changed almost overnight from impossible to become very responsive barking dogs.

One such case was that of Callum and Jeza. Callum was some three years older than Jeza and he would bark as a warning of any presence. After giving due warning of the visitor, he would be told to be quiet. Jeza grew up in this environment; she did not need to bark and there was no way that we could get her to do so. The 'be quiet' command to Callum also inhibited Jeza. However, within a few weeks of Callum's departure into the next world, Jeza took over the guarding role and started to bark at any person approaching the house or the car. She was then taught to 'speak on command'.

Puppy Caro joined our family and, although he was an independent character, he was happy to let Jeza do the barking for him. It was a long and patient struggle to get Caro to 'speak on command'. When Jeza finally followed Callum, Caro then took over the protective role and elected

With check chain in hand
Caro is induced to speak.

himself as guardian of our property.

Isla then joined the family as a puppy and as a junior she is already quite pleased to give Caro vocal backing when there is a need to give notice of an approaching visitor.

A dog cannot be made to speak if he does not wish to, and he will not give voice when requested if he does not understand what is wanted. The procedure for teaching a dog to speak when required is to praise him whenever he barks of his own volition. The reason for barking is of secondary importance. Encourage him with 'That's a good boy, Ben, *speak*' and repeat this phrase as often as you wish so long as he is speaking. However, five to ten seconds or so is long enough at any one time.

Make use of natural situations when your dog seems to have a reason for barking, but where possible create situations which, in themselves, will encourage him to bark. Consider yourself fortunate if you have an easy dog to train. On the other hand, you may have a dog which is unlikely to be a speaking candidate, or your past objection to his barking may have been so successful that you have created too big a hurdle to be cleared. A squeaky toy or some suitable article which makes a noise can be a very useful aid, especially for the more advanced exercise of detection and indicating the source of a presence. I find that the clink of a metal-link check chain in my hand is ideal. The check chain together with a ball can be useful, the chain to make the noise and the thrown ball to be the reward. If the noise in the hand coincides with the barking as well as the verbal encouragement, the noise can eventually replace the verbal encouragement.

A frequent problem is that of terminating a period of barking. Many a dog will bark but almost as many handlers have difficulty in regaining silence. Some who are successful in terminating a barking session suppress the activity to such an extent that the dog fails to 'indicate a presence'.

To obtain the correct balance give your dog the opportunity to bark when he wishes and with the degree of encouragement which suits the occasion. After a suitable period, say five to ten seconds, make it clear that you want him to stop. Make your directive as clear and as loud as you wish; your voice can be louder and more demanding than his. *'Ben, enough!'* repeated with strength should be sufficient, but do not accept failure. A few seconds of silence should be followed by encouragement to start barking again with 'That's a good boy, Ben, *speak*'. Another five to ten seconds of barking will help to counter your very demanding instruction to stop when required. When you can successfully get your dog to speak on command then fall into silence on demand, you will have created a situation of control. Speaking as part of the guarding activity, with a controlled termination, can then be perfected without inhibiting the dog on future guarding occasions.

Acceptance of a presence

To give warning of somebody approaching is a fundamental necessity for a guarding function, but it will be appreciated that on the majority of occasions that somebody will have no criminal intent. That person is just an innocent visitor or possibly the agent of a delivery or commercial service. In essence it is a person who is going about in a lawful manner and is entitled to a courteous reception. Thus we have the situation where there are occasions when it is advisable to ensure that a dog takes a protective stance when somebody approaches, but on recognition of a legitimate visitor the dog should be prepared to accept the presence of the person who has been 'cleared' by his handler.

It is the attitude of both the handler and the visitor which should control the dog's reaction. A pleasant and friendly attitude from each should result in a relaxed response from the dog. However, any sign of belligerence from either handler or visitor should result in an attentive canine response with a controlled preparedness for action. This type of response will be discussed in the next section.

Any sign of an aggressive canine response without due cause must be terminated immediately, this situation being similar to that of a dog which continues to bark beyond the call of duty. The handler must act in a positive and clear manner. If the aggressive attitude is minimal then 'Ben, enough!' should be sufficient to control the situation. However, the more aggressive canine response must be dealt with *very* firmly, resulting in a complete submission to your requirements.

To obtain the correct response it may be necessary to act very forcibly. Your dog should of course be wearing a collar, so you can slip your left hand between the collar and his neck (if he is wearing a check chain, take the active ring in your right hand). Tighten the collar (or chain) and twist with your left hand. Your knuckles will dig into the dog's neck muscles and this will be extremely unpleasant for him. Use the degree of pressure which is required to achieve your objective and at the same time give a very strong verbal reprimand. Three seconds of pressure is long enough – remember that you are choking your dog, but aggression must be countered effectively by controlled aggression. If three seconds of pressure is not long enough, this indicates that your own aggressive stance does not have sufficient strength.

Immediately the canine aggression is under control, put your dog into the down position and make him stay in that position until any short-term business with the visitor has been concluded. If the business is to take longer than five minutes or so, it may be advisable, after two minutes at the down, to put your dog into another area where attention to him is not required.

It is important to remember that praise must always be given when the response you require has been achieved. Also that repeated suppression of aggressive or unnecessary protective canine activities can inhibit a dog's protective reactions when they *are* required. It may therefore be necessary to create situations where the desired protective instincts are encouraged with good reason. The dog will then be able to discriminate and learn to react correctly to the situation.

Objection to a presence

There will be occasions when a visitor or an approaching person falls into the 'undesirable' category and the back-up from a dog gives the handler confidence to face the situation. If wisdom prevails on the part of the undesirable character, an ugly or otherwise unmanageable scene can be prevented.

Natural opportunities for protective training are likely to be very few and far between and it will probably be necessary to carry out training during mock situations to simulate suitable conditions. It is preferable to use a person who is not a good friend of the dog, although some dogs enjoy the aggravated rapport between friends and join in with their own brand of mock aggression.

Either yourself or your visitor can show displeasure at the meeting between the pair of you and the verbal aggression can be varied in order to monitor the response from your dog. Encouragement can be given to the dog by excited remarks such as 'You watch him, Ben' at the first signs of a positive response. Encouragement which is too enthusiastic may well create an over-reaction from your canine guardian so care must be taken to ensure that reactions are properly controlled.

Changing the role of the instigator of the aggressive attitude can be applied: on some occasions the handler can initiate the verbal aggression and on others the visitor can lead the way. This will give the dog the background and experience for the real thing when it occurs.

Control must be maintained at all times. Although attachment to a lead can be useful in training, a *complete* dependence on the lead indicates a failure on your part to control the situation. If there is a danger of the situation getting out of control, the methods recommended under the previous section, ACCEPTANCE OF A PRESENCE, should be applied.

Some dogs may require the introduction of physical aggression to induce a positive stance on their part. A bit of pushing with verbal abuse between the aggressor and the handler can change a dog from a mild-mannered companion to a very attentive protector. However, much thought and consideration must be given before venturing into this field. Your dog may not be a suitable candidate, you may not be a suitable handler and your helper or 'criminal' may not have the experience or ability to bring a dog out in a manner which is suited to the situation. This advancement in training is more in keeping with the build-up for MAINTAINING CONTACT with an intruder and will be fully discussed under that heading.

Detecting a presence and indicating the source

Detecting and locating the concealed intruder is the next phase of the training programme with the indication of the location as a natural follow-up. Although most dogs will find it natural to be aware of an unseen intruder and have the ability to locate his position, the dog's indication to the handler may not be sufficient to attract the latter's attention. These three factors – detecting, locating, indicating – are so closely related that they can be treated as one for training purposes.

Firstly, it is necessary to recognise and reiterate the importance of the dog's senses, also decide which of these senses are likely to play an important role under certain circumstances or conditions.

The sense of sight is probably the least important until the intruder has been located and we can, therefore, dismiss the dog's eyes as a major presence-detecting organ, although certainly useful as an indicator.

The sense of smell is extremely important and is of the highest value in detecting the scent of an intruder when the wind or draughts are in the appropriate direction. If the scent is not floating towards the dog he has no hope of detecting the intruder's presence. If the latter has passed through

Detecting and indicating
requires versatility and
experience.

Caro has detected an intruder and is indicating his presence.

the area in which the dog is positioned he will certainly detect the scent and should, within reason, have the ability to follow it and so find the intruder. The dog's ability to differentiate between scents and, with experience, to follow a line ensures that his nose is his principal detecting organ.

The sense of hearing is another important factor although its full value will come to the fore only under relatively quiet conditions. A smothered cough, a slight shuffle of feet, a creaking door hinge or floorboard, the snap of a twig are all give-away sounds which may not be noted by the human ear but can gain the attention of a dog.

The vibration from movement which is relatively silent can be felt by a dog and will set him on the alert.

The presence of an intruder when noted by one of the dog's senses will promptly activate all the other senses and result in the dog applying those appropriate to the situation and to the required degree.

So we have the situation of the dog being aware of a presence. Now we consider circumstances which go well beyond the scope of the domestic pet in his own home. The situation could involve a Parks Security dog being sent to flush out some unpleasant character who is reported to be hiding in the bushes, or to find a missing child who may be lying injured at an out-of-the-way spot. It could involve a Security dog on duty within some industrial, warehousing or sales premises where the variety of hiding places can be so numerous and unusual that a group of human searchers could easily miss an intruder, but a trained dog would find it to be the simplest of tasks. Or it could involve a gamekeeper or waterbailiff and his guard dog which will be alert to any movement, noise or scents which tell him of the presence of another party within his domain. Again, in this training exercise it is the mock intruder or our training 'criminal' who are the central characters.

It is assumed that the dog has been taught to speak on command and will respond to a particular noise inducement. For the purpose of describing the training routines it is presumed that the click of a check chain has been used to stimulate the speak, although other means of audible inducements will do. We must now make sure that your dog is going to speak on finding the hidden intruder.

Whilst your dog is on the lead, have the intruder excite him from a distance. This should produce a strong barking reaction. Immediately this has been achieved, have your intruder run away and quickly hide – but let your dog see him enter the hiding place. This can be behind a door, up a tree, in a packing case or some other convenient place. Time may be of the essence; too long a delay can cause a dramatic loss of interest. Suggest a maximum distance of 50 yards initially with an immediate release to the hiding place as soon as the intruder is out of sight. You can either run with the dog pulling you on the lead or let him off the lead so that you can follow at a suitable pace.

It is preferable that your intruder be in a position where he can observe without being seen by the dog: the door slightly ajar, a peep-hole in the packing case. If the dog does not make directly for the hiding place there has not been sufficient stimulation or there has been too long an interval

Chisum watches an intruder go into hiding . . .

. . . then follows up with purpose.

between the initial stimulation and the release of the dog.

The intruder may remain silent until found or he can make noises to help maintain an excited interest. Only he can judge what degree of incitement is required to achieve a good barking response when found but out of sight. The intruder who is hiding up a tree may not be out of sight but having the dog look up to find him and then to bark is success in itself. This response will certainly have its value during more advanced training.

However, total success at this stage is when the dog, on locating the intruder, barks without any encouragement. But to maintain a ten-second spell of continuous attention and barking may require support from the hidden intruder. A solid foundation of barking at this early stage will prove its value when more sustained searching is required to locate an intruder.

During this period of training the principal stimulus must come from the intruder, although a little gentle back-up from the handler will help to let the dog know what to expect if he does not see the intruder disappear from sight. This back-up can be in the form of an excited question 'Where is he? Are you going to find him, son?' and on release a positive 'Go and find him, son!'

On finding and barking with continuous enthusiasm for a suitable period, the intruder should be told by the handler to come out, the latter using an aggressive tone which will help to keep the dog alert.

On emerging from his hiding place the intruder should ensure that the dog maintains an attentive and vocal attitude for a further ten seconds or so. (This forms an introduction to maintaining contact with the intruder.)

The handler should then take the article of attraction from the intruder and terminate the sequence with a game, a thrown ball or some such play toy.

Vary the hiding places in this exercise. At this stage always let the dog see the intruder disappear from sight. The handler should keep his position after releasing the dog and wait until the animal has located the intruder and started barking before moving up to give moral support.

The foregoing theme will be developed into the more advanced quarter and searching exercise in a later section of the book.

Maintaining contact and keeping an intruder at bay

There is little value in having a dog indicate the presence of an intruder if he will not remain in contact and keep the unwelcome visitor from walking away. The same principle is at stake when finding a missing person who may well be injured or exhausted and, therefore, quite immobile. The dog must stay in the vicinity of that person and continue barking to attract his handler to the spot.

One is not in the position to witness how an operational police dog functions on active service but the patrol routine in the Working Trials Police Dog Stake gives good guidance as to the effectiveness of police dogs and also civilian dogs.

Caro turns to his handler and takes his attention from the intruder.

Many dogs have the tenacity to keep an intruder or criminal at bay for a good period of time but it has been noted that on occasions a competing dog will keenly go out, quarter and search for a hidden person, bark – then look for his handler. This is an indication of excessive moral support from the handler during training or of ineffective 'criminals' or intruders, where time and effort has not been taken to consolidate on the most elementary principle of maintaining contact.

In a practical situation a hidden intruder will do his best to remain perfectly still and silent; in fact, he may be too frightened to move. There are numerous situations where a dog or the handler can expect no assistance in maintaining contact. It is the skill of the training intruder which develops a dog into a persistent canine attendant. This skill cannot be gained from the written word, only from the developed experience of listening and watching a dog; of the intruder acting when the dog is beginning to lose interest or being distracted by some event which should be ignored.

When the dog's attention never wavers from the location of a hidden intruder without prompting from intruder or handler for some twenty seconds, he has reached a standard of attentiveness which will give the handler sufficient time to arrive at the scene and ensure that the hidden intruder is positively located.

We now come to the stage of ensuring that an intruder, who is in view of the dog, will remain in that position until the handler takes control of the situation.

Caro ensures that the intruder will not move.

Discounting the training for protection work, we are here dependent on the intruder's fear of the situation. He does not know if the dog is going to bite or not. The dog is barking and looks aggressive and this will be sufficient to deter movement on the part of those who are caught in compromising situations. At the moment we shall rely on this fear or lack of knowledge to keep the intruder at bay.

To maintain sighted contact depends on the skill of the training intruder in knowing what movements or sound to make, be it a jingle of coins in his pocket or a clicking noise of the vocal chords. It could be a combination of movement, noise and vibration by means of a stamping foot. The combinations are considerable and a good intruder or 'criminal' will know how and when to use them to maintain canine attention.

During this entire training exercise the handler should be maintaining a profile to suit the situation. He will become the trigger which sets off the searching pattern with his 'Where is he? Are you going to find him, son?' He must also read the actions of the intruder and become the controller if the dog is reacting too strongly or when the routine is terminated.

A dog who gets 'high' on this kind of work requires a strong voice which may in other, ordinary, circumstances ruin his character. Excesses cannot be tolerated from the dog and if these occur both intruder and handler must accept responsibility.

7 Training for Protection Duties

Self defence and prevention of escape

This is probably the most critical chapter of all. We begin now to draw very much on the dog's courage; he must be able to stand up for himself and to protect his handler. This may involve an attack on him with weapons, be it a pick-axe handle, a cycle chain or a gun. He must be able to avoid physical attacks but keep the 'criminal' from running away; when necessary, he must be able to turn defence into attack, to use his own principal weapon – his teeth.

Training the dog to bite and hold, to create the opportunity for him and for the dog to understand when to take it as the situation demands, requires drastic action. The right arm is the target and preferably just above the wrist. To gain and maintain that hold so long as the 'criminal' resists, but to

The full protection suit.

let go immediately resistance has terminated, is the aim. The complete build-up for protection work, often called 'manwork', is based on this ability to bite cleanly in the right place and to hold as long as necessary.

A good and safe protection dog is an asset to the community, but without care, consideration and attention to detail there are dangers. Again I emphasise that responsibilities must be recognised; the dog must be suitable material for training, the handler must be resolute in his approach, and the training 'criminal' must be suitably experienced, particularly in regard to the early stages of training. Each of these factors is a link in the chain of competence and safety. One weak link spells danger and the dog can become a liability instead of an asset.

Controlled aggression

Arousing the aggressive instincts within many dogs is quite simple, although with some this instinct requires to be triggered off before any meaningful reaction can be expected.

Consideration must be given to age as many young dogs have been ruined by encouraging or demanding the application of aggressive instincts at too early an age.

A trainer friend was very badly bitten and required extensive facial surgery because of an unexpected attack at an obedience training club meeting. The offender was an eight-month-old German Shepherd puppy which was being brought in for the first time. The owner was having problems but he conveniently omitted to tell the trainer of the real reason for joining the class. This owner had been training his *puppy* to protect him and had encouraged the first signs of aggressiveness. By the time this puppy was eight months old he could not control the situation.

One of my own German Shepherds was about nine months old when one day a situation developed where one would expect the protective instincts to come to the fore. However he stood placidly by my side as a heated situation developed. I made no attempt to trigger off the dormant instinct but watched for reactions; none were forthcoming. This same dog developed in his own time and with the basic training he received he now enjoys heated banter as a prelude to some active protection work.

Encouraging the protective instincts in a young puppy can be very damaging to his character and consideration must be given to the introduction of serious training before a puppy reaches his first birthday. Too many youngsters are ruined by an early introduction or excessive exposure to protection work. Training skill and knowledge is paramount because a dog's adult character is a reflection of earlier considerations. However, fun training can start with a puppy beyond the teething stage, but *be kept at that level* until he is mentally prepared to accept his responsibilities.

A tug of war between a dog and his handler, also selected friends, is the best introduction. In this way he can be taught by encouragement to bite, hold and pull.

Chisum training with the sack. (See also p. 106)

Chisum shows his tenacity.

Caro being used to entice youngsters to take an interest.

An old cardigan or a piece of sacking will fill the bill. Most dogs enjoy a little tease to bite at such an article. An old cardigan can be used to start with, followed by progression to a piece of sacking and then eventually a piece of tarpaulin or sailcloth. However, closely woven sailcloth can be difficult for an inexperienced dog to hold, especially when training develops to a covered dummy arm. It is, therefore, important that the dog has developed the tenacity to hold with great determination before introducing the more difficult materials.

When teasing the dog with the sacking he must always seem to be winning until human resistance ceases. Let him win easily to start with, make it fun, laugh and kid him along. Let go of the sacking when he is holding firmly then immediately give him great praise. Gradually increase the resistance from your own end so that he must work harder. Growl to let him feel that it is more of dog against dog than dog against man. As his confidence increases, your resistance can be stepped up until it is a real tug-of war with great determination at each end, but all the time allowing the dog to gain a little ground. He is winning.

During all of this activity, the sacking should initially be held in both hands (although some dogs prefer a single-handed approach) then developed into the right-handed holding of the sacking. It may well be natural for right-handed people to do this but the naturally left-handed person should also develop into the right-handed approach. As training progresses it is the right arm which should be the focus of attack, this being the usual weapon-carrying hand. However, the normally left-handed training 'criminal' can have advantages as his free left arm can be more accurate in his own defensive tactics.

When a dog has developed a reasonable degree of tenacity you should, on occasions, maintain your grip but without resistance. At the same time demand that he lets go using an extremely firm 'leave'. If he continues to hold, follow up immediately with any verbal abuse necessary to achieve the desired reaction. He must be taught to let go *the instant* you utter the firm 'leave' so verbal abuse to achieve your requirements may be a necessity in the earlier stages. Physical abuse is not acceptable and even consideration of it means that you have allowed the dog to take control. If you have allowed the situation to develop where verbal abuse is not sufficient then let go, but on future occasions terminate the exercise before the dog gets so 'high', to ensure that he understands that lack of resistance on your part plus the command to 'leave' means just that.

A few seconds after you have commanded him to leave and have instantly obtained your objective, start the game again but this time allow your dog to win by releasing the sacking and allowing him go away with his prize. Every time he wins give your dog praise and every time he responds to your 'leave' command be equally generous with your praise.

When a friend takes on the function of the tug-of-war opponent a little encouragement by yourself from time to time may be of value but your dog should not depend on it. A commencing, encouraging command such as 'You get it, son' will help at a later stage to trigger off the full attacking sequence. However, your friend should not give commands to leave. The friend should carry on with your routine by allowing the dog to win most of the time, but on the occasions when he plans to hold without resistance you must be prepared to command your dog's *immediate* release of the sacking and again apply verbal abuse if the response is not quick enough. Repeat the tug of war but this time allow the dog to win hands down and get away with his prize.

Tara's determination to hold on.

Once this stage has been reached, the dog's holding ability will have developed considerable strength. A dog with tenacity will hold the sacking with such a strong grip that he can be swung off the ground.

A dummy can now be made up to represent the forearm of the person to be attacked. A centre of good thick rope is ideal but a wooden centre can be used. Suitable padding of carpet underfelt or some such material can be included with a tight covering of sacking. At a later stage this covering can be changed to sailcloth. A loop of strong thick cord can be attached to one end to facilitate hand holding so that the trainer can have greater freedom of movement. The use of this dummy is just an extension of the original loose sacking.

Some dogs tend to be biters rather than holders and will make a succession of bites rather than one good take and hold. The good holders may on occasion require a second or third bite to get a firm hold if the dummy is not suited to an easy grip for that dog or that stage of training.

The use of a sailcloth dummy to induce a good bite.

The biters can be encouraged to hold by using a dummy covered with sacking (later with sailcloth) with the addition of a long piece of strong nylon cord bearing a holding loop at the free end. The end attached to the dummy is thrown over a bar or the branch of a tree some 10 feet or more from the ground.

Encouraging a good determined bite without the use of a 'criminal'.

With the handler controlling the line, the dummy can be made to swing at varying heights, also pulled out of reach of the dog when this suits your requirements. The dummy can be used to tease the dog a little and when he grabs hold of it he can be enthusiastically encouraged to retrieve it back to you. You are in a position to apply as much or as little tension on the cord as suits your purpose. As he holds and pulls the dummy closer you must give a little ground to let him know he is winning, but he has to work for it. This is a super game and can greatly toughen up the dog's bite, his tenacity and holding power without involving another human being.

There is one difficult type of biter and that is the dog which goes in from underneath. He twists his head in a manner which makes it difficult for him to hold the sacking or dummy which is held at both ends. This approach is possibly an inherited throwback from the days of the pack dog hunting for food. The animal of prey which went in for the target's throat had to turn his head round to get a hold from underneath; this action would help to bring the prey down whilst others in the pack attacked from the rear. Unfortunately, this possibly inherited approach to biting is a slight handicap for today's protection dog. I do not know of an easy cure but a good 'criminal', by the way he presents his right arm, can make the straightforward bite more obvious to the dog.

Training to this stage can be carried out by the handler but an experienced training 'criminal' should also be introduced to the routine.

The uninterested dog

There are certain dogs which show no interest in the excitement from attempted tug-of-war playing. They may not be suited to this kind of work, but on the other hand they may require some form of trigger to set the dormant protection instinct going. However, great care must be taken to ensure that any methods of triggering this instinct do not have undesirable side effects.

An incorrect approach can create an overaggressive dog or an apprehensive attitude when somebody approaches, particularly from the rear. Most triggers are best left to the expert training 'criminal' who has had an opportunity to study the dog and is able to assess responses and reactions. He can tailor his approach to suit the particular dog.

The furtive approach with growling noises from the 'criminal' may be sufficient to alert the dog and prepare him for a flick from a piece of sacking which could make him grab for it. The furtive approach together with a quick dart in to nip the loose skin in front of the upper thigh at the groin can be very effective. Nipped correctly and the dog will whip his head round quickly to bite the offending hand. An available piece of sacking round the wrist can attract the bite and thus create a breakthrough.

This approach can also be applied to dogs which are accustomed to a tug of war but require a little attention-getting activity in order to obtain an attentive reaction to a lurking stranger. This technique can be re-introduced at any time to overcome any failure to pay attention to suspicious situations.

On to the arm

The change to the arm from loose sacking or a dummy is easily carried out. The sacking can be wrapped round the arm or the dummy tied to the arm. However, it may be preferable to start with the sacking.

Treat this stage as a continuation of the tug-of-war game with your dog being very keen to grab the sacking. Again it is a case of letting the dog feel that he is winning. Initially the sacking can be wrapped in such a manner that the arm can slide out in order to let your dog free with his prize.

He should not be allowed freedom with the sack too often or he may be easily distracted by the release of surplus clothing in a genuine situation. I recall Callum, my GSD, as a relatively inexperienced dog competing in the Police Dog Stake where we were carrying out the escort exercise. The 'criminal' took off his bonnet to throw it away. The bonnet in flight caught Callum's attention and he left his post to catch it. This gave the 'criminal' the opportunity to turn and attack me. I shouted Callum's name and he immediately turned and responded with his own attack on the 'criminal's' arm. However, the bonnet in flight across his line of vision had distracted him from his prime function – that of escorting a 'criminal'.

Some dogs can lose a little confidence when they are presented with the sacking on the arm. They may feel that they are going to hurt the person

A training 'criminal' prepares his arm.

under attack. With such dogs it may be advisable to wrap the sacking round the arm whilst the animal is holding on, leaving a tail of sacking available until the dog is prepared to take a full bite on the forearm.

A good strong bite can and will hurt, even with protection. It helps considerably at all stages to bandage the biting area of the arm with a crepe bandage. Training 'criminals' recognise that they will finish a good session with a certain amount of bruising and one often finds these trainers proudly showing off the results of working with a good firm-biting dog.

Protection equipment

On progressing from the stage of loose sacking or the dummy, proper arm-protection equipment is necessary. I use made-up canvas sleeves lined with carpeting or layers of carpet felt and of a length which will cover from hand to elbow. A loop of strong tape or cord attached inside can give a good holding grip to ensure that the sleeve does not get pulled off unless you wish to release it. This is an adequate intermediate form of protection before progressing to the leather sleeve.

Custom-made leather sleeves are available. These afford greater protection and are usually less bulky. These sleeves can be hidden inside

The value of a well-padded sleeve as Rio takes a bite.

the coat sleeve, thus creating a less artificial situation for the dog. Dogs can become 'padding happy' when they will only attack if they can see the protection which is being used.

The full protection sleeve of canvas or leather can be introduced at any suitable time during the period of training, but any difficulty due to the nature of the protection equipment must be recognised and steps taken to eliminate this problem.

Physical agitation and tests of courage

Attacks from the 'criminal' whilst the dog is holding the arm can greatly reinforce the dog's tenacity. To kick gently with the side of the foot at the dog's side is one way of testing the animal's determination to hold. A little more force in that side-footed kick can be used as the dog accepts this form of retaliation. It will teach the dog to be watchful and avoid the force of a blow whilst maintaining a firm grip of the arm. Obviously, the toe of the boot or shoe must *never* be used and the application of the kick must be in a manner which cannot possibly cause any physical damage.

A whippy stick can also be used; a fine garden cane or a slender and supple branch from a bush or tree is the type of weapon which can sting when used against a dog's fore-shoulder. This can act in a similar manner to

The gentle kick.

that of the jockey with his whip. A determined dog will become immune to the stinging pain from the use of such a weapon but it can increase his determination to hold on. He will also learn to avoid the whippy stick.

A stout weapon must *not* be used. The purpose of the whippy stick or the side of the foot is to increase the dog's holding power and to create a certain respect for such action where he will be forever watchful and will take avoiding action whilst not on the arm.

Increased determination on the part of the dog can be attained by a limited amount of baiting whilst he is on the lead. Again the whippy stick can be used in a menacing manner without actually having to hit the dog.

You should have your dog on a good length of lead. A police-type lead at its full length is suitable, i.e. about 6 feet in length. The collar should be of a type which does not tighten on the dog's neck. A leather collar or a shortened check chain with lead attached to the dead ring would be satisfactory. The dog should not be able to pull his head out and a quick release is essential.

Some agitated banter between yourself and the 'criminal' could on occasions be used to trigger off a protective stance from the dog. The menacing attitude of the 'criminal' with his stick being swung about to indicate an attacking situation will bring out a threatening approach from the dog where he is allowed to lunge forward at the end of the lead. So long as the menacing attitude is maintained the dog is encouraged to threaten the 'criminal' and it is only the attachment to the lead which prevents him from getting close enough to bite.

It is the 'criminal's' responsibility to make sure that he is sufficiently fleet of foot to avoid being bitten. You, as the handler, should also maintain a stance which prevents any uncontrolled movement on the part of the dog which could put the training 'criminal' at a disadvantage. To give ground bit by bit, to follow a slowly retreating but menacing 'criminal' is another matter. In this instance it can help to give your dog confidence by winning.

Some 'criminals' encourage the handler to allow the dog to bite whilst on the lead, then to check with the lead on the termination of the 'criminal's' resistance. I feel that this approach is a short-cut to controlled biting and indicates a lack of groundwork which can result in a lack of control during practical off-lead situations.

The conclusion of each menacing attack should always be the complete deflation of the 'criminal'. He should cease resistance by standing still with his arms by his side in a completely relaxed manner. The dog must respond in a similar manner. A failure to obtain immediate control with the command 'Enough' or 'Finish' indicates excessive agitation from the 'criminal' for the particular stage of training, or an inept controlling response from the handler, or even a lack of basic training. The cause must be analysed and fully rectified before continuing with this type of agitated training.

Physical agitation can provide very effective tests of courage, especially when accompanied by aggressive shouting from the 'criminal'. Some dogs can stand up to physical agitation but aggressive shouting, the banging of tins and such like have caused them to retreat; some may even finally run away.

Various noises should, therefore, be brought into the act of agitation – but only by degrees, in order to ensure that this additional element is not only accepted by the dog but helps to stimulate his aggressive response. The use of a gun is also a test of courage, but it can also be used as a test of mental stability where the sound of the weapon being fired (or a similar sound) does not trigger off a canine aggressive reaction.

Although the experience of physical agitation and baiting together with tests of courage must be treated with intelligence and care, this form of training can save a working dog's life and that of his handler.

Searching and disarming a criminal

An armed criminal must be rendered harmless. To allow you to perform the function of body searching or disarming the criminal he must respect and fear your dog's presence. To carry out this operation you must be freed to act independently of your dog and yet know that he will act in the appropriate manner if the criminal decides to attack you or to run away.

Your dog should be put into the down position at a distance of about two

Bringing an intruder into the open.

Searching an intruder for weapons.

or three paces from the 'criminal' and at his right-hand side. You should always make sure that you never get directly between the 'criminal' and your dog. This could create a blind spot for the dog while an intelligent 'criminal' could take advantage and attack you. When the dog can watch every possible movement of the 'criminal' he is more likely to stay alert, watching and waiting for a possible wrong move. Whilst you are carrying out a body search the 'criminal' should watch your dog for any signs of inattention. Any such signs should result in action from the 'criminal', either in the form of an attack or a break away. This action will help to ensure that your dog maintains a vigilant outlook at all times.

The chase or pursuit and detention

The build-up of enthusiasm for the bite and to hold on is the basis for a good purposeful chase. The dog will already have been taught to go for the 'criminal's' right forearm and it is the running 'criminal's' function to ensure that the arm is readily available to be taken in flight. Otherwise an overexcited or careless dog may go for any part of the body which is available. When the dog has become more experienced the 'criminal' can then hold his arm in a more natural manner and know that the dog will still make a point of going for the (less obvious) target.

This part of the training routine is based on the use of a normal tone of voice when the handler is questioning the 'criminal'. At this stage the dog should be attentive but not aggressive in any way. In a practical situation

Fonz catches a running 'criminal'.

the 'criminal' could be an innocent person who may have inadvertently trespassed into a protected area. It is only when the banter becomes heated that the dog should consider that positive action may be required on his part.

Distance between yourself and the 'criminal' is dependent on the dog's enthusiasm for giving chase. Five to ten yards may be sufficient to start with, the dog being released as soon as the 'criminal' starts running away. A build-up to 100 yards or more between yourself and the 'criminal' would be advisable with a good running start by the 'criminal', before releasing your dog.

On catching the 'criminal' the dog should be prepared to hold on until you arrive on the scene. However, if the 'criminal' stops struggling the dog should automatically come off but remain on guard with his full attention on the 'criminal' until you arrive, carry out the body search (if necessary) and escort to complete the procedure of detaining the 'criminal'.

As control training is part of your dog's basic schooling you should be able to put him into the down position off the lead whilst the introductory banter is taking place. The dog must learn to stay down whilst the 'criminal' is running away and only take off after him when the release command comes from yourself.

This objective may result in some harsh words for your dog to ensure that he contains himself until he has been verbally released. However, a dog which is 'high' and enthusiastically awaiting the chase will accept such harshness, when it would not be acceptable at any other time.

In a genuine situation, mistakes can occur and the apprehended person may decide to run away through fear rather than guilt. When this has been realised by the handler, the dog must be stopped from going in for the bite.

This comes down to control through the voice, or a whistle if the dog has been trained for such a response.

This exercise is known as the 'running recall' where the dog is called back from a person in full flight, or the 'stand off' where the person stops running and stands still. With the running recall the dog should be stopped and return to the handler when recalled. It is acceptable, however, if the dog runs with the fleeing person so long as he makes no attempt to bite. In the case of the stand off the dog should circle the person and keep him there without attempting to bite until the handler arrives on the scene.

To call a dog off when he is going full out to stop a running criminal can be extremely difficult, especially with a good enthusiastic chase dog. To get a controlled call off without spoiling the enthusiastic chase requires a fine balance of control, enthusiasm and intelligent training. This is where basic control comes to the fore with instant and unquestioning responses during normal daily situations.

If your dog goes to chase another dog and you cannot stop him there is no hope of your achieving a running recall. If he is sniffing at some bush which has been used as another dog's convenience and fails to respond to your call, he is again unlikely to respond to the running recall.

Training under non-protection situations should be used to create the foundation of the running recall. The command to 'leave' can be used in all situations to stop your dog from carrying out the activity in question and it is important that his immediate attention be obtained. This is instantly followed by a recall or the command to stay and await your approach to him.

Appropriate situations can readily be set up to achieve success outside the protection scene.

(1) Have a member of your family call your dog from a distance and if necessary be running away at the same time. You release the dog when he is very keen to go.
(2) Have fun with a ball. Throw it a good distance and release your dog whilst the ball is moving. *NOTE*: Make sure the ball is big enough. Dogs can choke on small balls.

On each of these occasions release your dog to take up the chase, but on the very odd occasion call him to 'leave' and return to you. However, don't call him back too often or he will come to expect a recall and will not take up the chase with determination. The result could well be a lack of determination and a failure to catch the criminal during a practical situation.

It must be recognised that the further the dog is from you the less control you are likely to have. It is important to build up on success from a short distance, that is within 20 per cent of the total distance you wish to achieve. If the incentive to go is 50 yards away, stop your dog by the time he has covered 10 yards. With each degree of success, gradually increase the distance covered before calling the dog to stop and return to you. As already stated there is a very fine line between success and failure.

The stand off should be much easier to obtain. Your dog has already been trained to guard and stay with a stationary 'criminal'. The success of this training now becomes a crucial ingredient of the stand off. In training, the 'criminal' should initially stop and stand perfectly still when the dog is quite a distance away in order to give him plenty of time to weigh up the situation. As training progresses the distance between dog and 'criminal' when he stops can be reduced to the minimum.

A proper mix of chase and running recall or stand off must be carried out to achieve the determined chase and catch, yet be sure of the dog reacting correctly to the call off situation.

Training for the chase can be started at any time after the dog has started working with the 'criminal' and is taking a good clean and positive bite. Some dogs will progress quickly throughout the full protection work routine via the chase. However, the dangers related to handler control from a distance must be recognised with limitations being applied accordingly.

Escorting the criminal

The feature of escorting follows from a variety of possible circumstances. It could be the result of finding a hidden intruder or the capture after a chase, which would normally be followed by a body search.

For the escort the dog should walk at the handler's left side and up to a body length ahead of the handler. The handler should adjust his own distance so that the dog's head is just behind the 'criminal's' right side.

The dog's attention must not wander from the 'criminal' at any time and it is the 'criminal's' job to ensure that the dog remains attentive. Any sign of canine inattention should result in direct and sudden action from the 'criminal'. He can either break away or turn to attack the handler. Each training escort should include either a break away or an attack to give the dog a reward for his attentiveness.

The handler's principal function is to maintain the correct distance behind the 'criminal' and ensure that the dog does not become over-enthusiastic. As the dog is off the lead, verbal control may be required to ensure that the dog maintains his correct position.

The handler applies control whilst the 'criminal' maintains canine enthusiasm.

Your dog and the gun

Your dog's reaction to the gun will depend entirely on the circumstances in which it is used and these can be classified into two types of situation.

(1) Meaningless gunfire. This can be in an area of target practice; in the country when a shoot for game is taking place; or in the region of a bird scarer.

(2) An aggressive situation. When the gun is being pointed and fired at the dog or his handler.

To deal with normal every-day life when meaningless gunfire is taking place, or any other explosive noise which can be interpreted by the dog as gunfire, the dog should be conditioned to accept such noises without any undue reaction. He may wish to know where the noise has come from, but that should be the limit of his interest. This form of conditioning must be complete and satisfactory before any attempt is made to apply an aggressive situation which will bring out canine offensive instincts and any attack training which may be required of the dog.

The guns to be used can vary quite considerably. A starting pistol can be a good introduction, as can a service revolver, a gun dog dummy launcher or a twelve-bore shotgun; all have different types of explosive noises when triggered off. NOTE: Blank cartridges should *always* be used.

The dog should not be introduced to the noise of a gun from close range. Initial reaction must be tested from a distance, remembering that wind direction will also have an effect on the magnitude of the noise. Some 50 yards between dog and gun with the wind carrying the sound to him or 30 yards with the wind minimising the sound can be a good testing range. Adjustments can be made according to the dog's reaction.

During the conditioning spell it is advisable that the handler fires the gun then calls the dog to him. This teaches the dog to move towards the source of the noise rather than to run away from it. The firing of the gun is, therefore, best carried out when the dog is free and at a suitable distance away. Close-up shots must be avoided until the dog is guaranteed to react in a satisfactory manner.

Every time you fire the gun, get your dog in quickly for praise and make fun of the situation. It is irrelevant whether or not the dog sees the gun during the earlier stages, but he should be accustomed to seeing the gun *after firing* before there can be any introduction of aggressive situations involving the gun. Another party should now fire the gun from a reasonable distance and in a non-aggressive manner, thus familiarising the dog with a different situation.

Aggressive use of the gun should now be introduced, in conjunction with a protection set-up. Have your dog on the lead and your 'criminal's' arm suitably protected. The latter should apply threatening behaviour, waving of the arms and the shouting of abusive language to induce an attacking response from the dog. When the dog has been baited sufficiently and from a reasonable distance, about 10 paces, the 'criminal' points the gun at the dog. At this moment you release the dog to attack. As he is being released the 'criminal' fires a shot and then runs away. Your dog takes up the chase and detains the 'criminal'.

The distance between dog and 'criminal' can now be varied, and the 'criminal' can occasionally stand his ground when he fires the gun. The objective is to have your dog go into the attack, without hesitation, on release when threatened with a gun.

To obtain the correct balance between meaningless gunfire and aggressive situations a suitable mix should be developed after the aggressive sessions have been introduced.

Food refusal

Food refusal can save a guard or protection dog's life. A doped or poisoned piece of meat left in a convenient place or dropped in front of a dog is an easy and positive way of neutralising the animal.

It must be understood, however, that training for food refusal is very much against a dog's nature. He has no inherited instincts to help him ignore a morsel of food which tempts his palate.

By its very nature then, food refusal training is disagreeable for the dog. Unpleasant associations under particular circumstances are being created and this training must be done with great care to ensure that the dog understands what is required of him. The refusal of food, be it titbits or a meal, from anybody not *very* closely connected with the dog must be maintained at all times. To allow the dog to accept a titbit, even in your own presence, and then expect him to refuse food when on duty is quite unreasonable.

The handler does not teach his dog to refuse food. Practical assistance is required from a suitable outside source. An experienced aide, probably your training 'criminal', can be of help here. The handler is merely an onlooker and must accept the treatment his dog is going to receive at the hands of the helper.

Some years ago, when I was a novice in this business and with my first dog in Working Trials, we had graduated into our first Police Dog Stakes. On this occasion we had the misfortune to be running first competitor to work and had no chance of watching the patrol work routine. All the other work had been completed and my GSD, Quest, was in the lead. The dog which was in second place was a seasoned campaigner, he was already a Working Trials Champion and he could overtake my marks so easily on the final group of exercises. However, his handler was a real gentleman. We were chatting, the old hand and the novice, whilst the hides were being set up for the Quarter and Search exercise. The routine was developed in such a manner that, on finding the 'criminal', food would be thrown on to the ground to tempt the dog. As we were chatting this handler, without saying a word of warning to me, offered Quest a piece of the meat pie he was eating. Quest put his head forward to sniff at the food when any thought of taking it was knocked out of his head as the back of the handler's hand caught him across the nose. The whole episode took both the dog and myself by surprise and all the handler said was 'He won't touch food out there today.' This gentleman was quite correct and he was happy to finish in second place to a dog he thought deserved that little bit of help on the day.

As I have said before this particular training is unpleasant and you must assess the need for it before embarking on such a restrictive outlook.

Initially, have your helper(s) offer food whilst your dog is beside you and on the lead. The food should be offered by hand and any attempt by the dog to even sniff should be penalised with a slap over the nose and at the same time a shout from the 'criminal'. Any noise from his vocal chords will do so long as it is short and sharp. Now have the food dropped in front of the dog's nose with your helper ready to move in fast with a shout should the dog drop his head with the intention of sniffing it. The memory of the previous slap on the nose will make the dog heed the 'criminal's' quick movement and he will anticipate similar treatment.

Various foods can be used in this exercise – raw meat, a sandwich, a piece of cheese, a drink of milk, ice cream or even a hard-boiled egg; anything which is likely to take your dog's fancy.

More advanced training can include the placing of food on that area of ground being patrolled by the dog on the loose. Your helper can leave the food at various prearranged spots and he can be hidden, preferably where his scent will not reach the dog. The helper must maintain a vigilant watch on the food and any indication of the dog putting nose to food must be instantly countered by a shout from the helper and his appearance to give visual distraction. Your own participation should be limited to a little praise when your dog leaves the food and control of the dog if he considers any action against the non-aggressive helper.

Titbits for your dog from anybody except yourself should be avoided. Normal feeding should be restricted to specific times and places, also limited to members of the family or colleagues who may have to look after the dog during your absence.

8 Quartering for a Hidden Person

Introduction

This is an extension of the earlier section on DETECTING A PRESENCE AND INDICATING THE SOURCE. The dog is now taught to quarter a piece of ground, a building or an industrial yard in order to seek out a hidden person. That person may have criminal intent or be a missing person who could be lying injured in some obscure corner or unexpected location.

A properly trained dog should be able to work with the minimum of direction or control from his handler and be expected to cover the area of search to the left, to the right and in front of the handler. Distances of one hundred yards or more from the controlling influence of his handler can be a reasonable expectation.

As already discussed the senses of sight, sound and smell are the principal detecting and locating factors which become operative in recognising the presence of someone within the searching area. The ability to give voice is normally the means of indicating a find.

Although sight and sound of the hidden person will be fully utilised during the build-up of a searching routine, the principle of wind scenting will also be utilised to the full. The value of body scents from a hidden person should be appreciated and we must capitalise on a dog's unique ability to detect via his olfactory system.

As already stated the objective is to locate a missing person or a hidden criminal, and the dog sent out to quarter an area should react in a manner which suits the circumstances. In the case of a missing person the dog should give voice to let his handler know of the location. Although he should remain with his find he must not show signs of aggression which would cause concern to an innocent party. It must be recognised that the missing person could be a child or an elderly person who is likely to be in a distressed condition. On the other hand it could be a criminal who requires to be located and flushed out. The dog would, therefore, require to be vigilant, and be prepared to defend himself or prevent the escape until his handler is available to take control of the situation.

The earlier section of this book under the heading of DETECTING A PRESENCE AND INDICATING THE SOURCE (page 95) will have already created the foundation for the quartering routine. At this stage the dog should have the enthusiasm and ability to go to a single hiding place, locate the person, give voice and maintain contact.

To quarter in the open

A pattern for quartering should now be developed. The dog already knows, from his earlier training, that various types of landmarks may well conceal a person in hiding. However, less obvious hiding places may well be used. A criminal may use a ditch or a missing person could be lying in undergrowth just high enough for him to remain unseen.

To commence quartering, your dog should be prepared to move in the direction you wish to send him. He should also have the initiative to deviate from that line if a noise or an airborne scent indicates the presence of a person out of his direct line of movement. His senses will then act as a homing device which will lead him directly to the hiding place.

Your hidden intruder is still the principal controlling influence; when found he will react in a manner which ensures maintenance of the dog's attention. However, on occasions this intruder will be acting as an innocent missing person and on others he will pose as a hardened criminal. Although we continue to use the male gender, females can be used to simulate missing persons. Serious consideration should be given before using females for aggravation and protection work.

Until the routine has been fully developed your intruder should be watching for the release of your dog to find him and any indecision on the dog's part should be immediately countered by the intruder drawing attention to himself. This can be either by creating adequate noise, coming into view, or both, but only for sufficient time to achieve his objective.

The initial inducement should never be forgotten and the dog must be given the reward which persuaded him to go out with confidence and enthusiasm, i.e. finding his quarry.

When using fairly open ground for training select a field or other suitable area with points of cover. Some cover should be large enough to hide your intruder in a standing position, others with him in a crouched or sitting position, and yet others at ground level where your intruder can be out of sight until the dog is right on top of him. Your intruder can also be completely out of sight even when located by the dog.

I can recall one training exercise with SAS territorials where we had to find a soldier on military training ground. Locating the man was not difficult. By making good use of the wind direction, Callum, my GSD, quickly homed in on a particular gorse bush and barked to draw my attention. Although I could see nothing Callum persisted in his attention. The art of self-camouflage was excellent and only the soldier's movement to leave the hiding place revealed his presence to me.

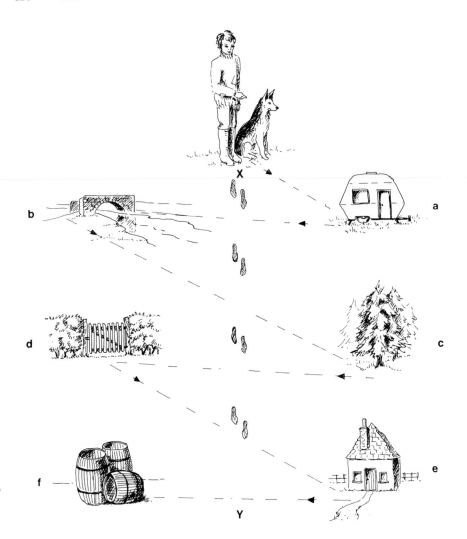

Pattern for quartering to find a missing person or concealed intruder.

The starting point and your base line should be right along the centre of the area to be quartered (this is indicated by the X – Y line in the diagram). Two hiding places should initially be selected, one to the right and the other to the left, with at least 50 yards to each side of the centre line to be quartered.

Whilst you are at your starting point with your dog, have the intruder walk round the edge and disappear behind hide A. It is preferable not to have a scent path between yourself and the hide now that you have developed beyond the elementary stages. The dog has been watching and he knows what is coming – it is a simple locate and indicate from a sighting. As soon as the intruder is out of sight release your dog to locate and give voice at his find. Rejoin your dog and reward him in the appropriate manner. Remember that this reward can be through intruder aggravation or fun with the check chain or some such play toy.

Walk back round the field with your dog and the intruder, then take the dog out of sight whilst the intruder returns round the field and conceals himself again behind hide A. When you have collected your dog and returned to your starting point release your dog with the trigger phrase he has grown to know 'Where is he? Go and find him, son.' Any indecision from the dog should bring an immediate reaction from the intruder to draw attention to himself. A satisfactory response should not be difficult to attain.

The next stage is to have your intruder move round to the other edge of the area to hide B whilst your dog is out of sight. You want him to believe that hide A is still occupied. Return to the starting point with your dog and release him in the direction of hide A. If you feel that your dog has caught the scent of the intruder's movement round hide B, move with your dog in the direction of hide A to ensure that he goes out in the desired direction. Your encouragement will help him on his way.

Your dog's quartering to hide A will be quite fruitless and as soon as he discovers the hide to be empty your watching intruder should come into view and make sufficient noise to draw the dog's attention. As soon as your dog reacts to the intruder the latter must immediately conceal himself and await the arrival of the dog to complete the training exercise. This should be sufficient for one training session.

The next training session should be a repetition of the first but the order in which the hides are used should be reversed. Start with hide B then change to hide A. The training sessions should be repeated, reversing the hides, until your dog is prepared to work the two hides in any order without knowing which is occupied. It is important that advancement to the next stage is withheld until the two-hides exercise is properly carried out.

The centre line (X – Y in the diagram) should be maintained as your base line during this and the more advanced stages. You should not deviate from the guide line until your dog has located the intruder and given voice. Remember that your intruder is in full control after your dog is released to quarter and search, and your job should be reasonably passive until the intruder has been located.

Although your role is mainly that of observer, a little verbal encouragement can be used whilst your dog is doing all the right things. However, any attempt on your part to *correct* him will eventually result in your playing a much more involved role with your dog backing you up, with possible failure to find any hidden intruders.

The location at hide C can now be added to the active hides with your dog quartering first to hide A and hide B, then your intruder drawing the dog's attention to the additional hide. With three hides your dog must be kept guessing; he will not know which active hide is in use until he checks it out. Each of the three hides must be used from time to time but the order of checking them out must be A or B first before hide C is checked. The fourth hide D should not be brought into active service until your dog is prepared to work the first three hides enthusiastically.

The procedure can gradually be developed until a total of half a dozen hides are being actively utilised. A change of venue will probably require a return to the original A and B hide procedure until your dog becomes familiar with the new surroundings. However, each change of venue will provide an invaluable increase in your dog's experience until the routine becomes second nature to him.

Wind direction can be important and it is your dog's ability to wind scent which will usually result in a find. To train in a direction where there are head or cross winds can have your dog locate the scent of your intruder earlier than intended. Any attempt at this stage to redirect him can only result in confusion.

Your intruder should always move round the perimeter of the quartering area when going to the first hide or from one hide to another. This will avoid leaving a single scent path for the dog to pick up. However, you could on occasions have your quartering area so contaminated with human scent that the intruder walking across the area would make no appreciable difference.

Although artificial hides have a decided value, natural hides should be used whenever available. To have your intruder hide above the level of the dog (such as up a tree or lying flat on the roof of a car) can only help to make a dog more versatile in his approach to quartering.

Building searches

There are many occasions when buildings require to be searched, particularly to locate a hidden intruder. It is important, therefore, when training, to ensure that the building is clear of all other people as the dog is not to be expected to differentiate between friend and foe.

Buildings can afford so many hiding places and some can be so unusual that an army of human searchers could fail to find a hidden intruder. It is remarkable how small a person can make himself when desperation controls his instincts and actions.

Choice of training sites will depend on availability. Farm buildings are ideal, especially when used in conjunction with quartering in the open. Derelict warehouses, factories or dwelling houses also offer opportunities for search training.

Start by having your intruder hide at a pre-arranged spot behind a door, a piece of machinery, in a cupboard or some such place. When you bring your dog into the vicinity of the hiding place have your intruder make his presence known, by sound or sight or both. Remember that your intruder is still the principal controlling influence and that your dog must be suitably rewarded for making this find.

A repeat search can now be carried out to the same hiding place, but this time from a spot further away and out of sight of the hiding place. Again release your dog with the trigger phrase 'Where is he?' It now becomes more difficult for your intruder to assess the dog's reaction. He is unlikely to be in a position to watch the dog and it may be advisable to have some sort of code between yourself and the intruder so that you can indicate to the latter when your dog requires a little help. He may find it necessary to give a cough, shuffle his feet or create some other movement to draw the dog's attention. In addition, scenting an intruder within a building can be more difficult than wind scenting in the open. The scent within a building becomes trapped and the area may well be filled with human scent and the dog may require to concentrate much more to locate the actual source of the scent.

Where possible, the same hiding place should be approached from different directions. This will give the dog a bit more experience before changing hides.

Two hiding places can now be used in different areas of the same building, or even two different rooms of a derelict house. Follow your dog to the hiding place which was originally in use. When he discovers it to be vacant, indicate to him the direction of the second hiding place. Use a tone which can be heard by your intruder so that he can draw attention to his new hiding place.

Progression to a third hiding place should only be considered when your dog is responding fully to the interchangeability of the first two hiding places. The build-up to additional hiding places can then be generated in the same manner as the application to open space quartering.

A new venue again means starting afresh until experience and enthusiasm ensure success when breaking fresh ground. The full value of experience will be evident by your dog's ability to cope with more difficult and demanding situations. Have him use his eyes and ears as well as his nose; the slightest movement or sound can be a giveaway and will help the dog to locate the hidden intruder. An intruder hiding in the rafters or on the top of a stack of packing cases can be missed by the novice dog but not by one which has learnt through experience.

9 Guarding and Protection Versatility

Introduction

Training routines can teach a dog the basic requirements of any guarding or protection function but variety creates versatility.

The domestic pet or the industrial watch dog will probably gain his limited, but sufficient, versatility through practical experience and is unlikely to require any special training beyond the details given in the earlier chapters. However, the controlled free ranging of a guard dog or protection dog to locate a hidden intruder or a missing person does require greater versatility. The application of the various features of protection work also benefit from a versatile approach.

No two practical situations are identical. The weather, the wind, the noise, the locations and the number of people involved all contribute to the innumerable variations of situation which can be encountered by a dog. Fortunately most dogs, particularly of the working breeds, are quick to learn and unless we stifle their natural resourcefulness by stereotyped training they generally prove to be very adaptable and versatile.

Quartering situations

Dogs which are limited by the areas in which they are likely to be searching may only require training to cover the special circumstances prevailing within these areas.

A dog on guard within a scrap-car yard may be required to crawl through or under car shells; he may even be required to jump from one car roof or bonnet to another; he may also be required to negotiate engines, gear boxes, axles and such like with swiftness and dexterity that can only come from experience within his patch.

An industrial location might have packing cases, machinery and all sorts of odds and ends either neatly stacked or distributed in apparent disarray with innumerable hiding placess.

A warehouse or multiple retail outlet can give a completely different set of conditions where hiding places can be so numerous that the trainer's ingenuity is required to give the dog sufficient experience to cover all eventualities.

Dogs which are used by security firms, police or government departments may well require the versatility to cover *any* type of site and must therefore be suitably adaptable.

Agility

Some circumstances may require canine agility to the extent that special training is advisable. The Long, Clear and Scale jumping for Working Trials will certainly give a dog the keenness and ability to negotiate most obstacles. The basic objectives of these three jumps are:

(a) *Long jump* – To have the dog clear a nine feet long spread of boards to create length of jump rather than height.

(b) *Clear jump* – To have the dog clear a hurdle which is three feet in height.

(c) *Scale jump* – To have the dog scale a six feet vertical wall of wooden planks, also to return back over the scale as required.

A Dobermann (Koriston Pewter Strike of Doberean C.D.Ex. U.D.Ex. W.D.Ex. T.D.Ex.) taking the long jump.

The same dog flying over the clear jump.

The full requirements and training routines for these agility applications are given in *Training the German Shepherd Dog* (Pelham Books, 1977).

Versatility with other types of obstacle is an advantage and can be attained by training to the requirements of the Kennel Club Agility Tests. The negotiation of tunnels, hoops, plank walks and various other tests are included within the routines. Full training and construction details are given in *The Agility Dog* (Canine Publications, 1981).

Protection work

Application of the training described in Chapter 7 will have created a sound protection dog but the training to date has only covered the involvement of a single intruder or 'criminal'. Practical situations can have two or more participants with criminal intent, so the training should be extended to cover the involvement of at least two 'criminals'.

As for the earlier stages these training 'criminals' should be well experienced both as individuals and as a team to ensure that they create situations

Caro takes the scale jump.

which will give both dog and handler the experience they require.

It is important that both dog and handler can operate with a degree of independence but be prepared to concentrate on a single 'criminal' if the safety of either one is in doubt. In other words, a dog should be prepared to abort an attack or pursuit if his handler is in danger and requires assistance. A two-against-one situation can guarantee a capture with relative safety and a divided effort should be treated with caution.

Two or three training 'criminals' can easily highlight the weaknesses in a protection partnership. They can then proceed to act in a manner which will create strength and confidence in both handler and dog.

Working Trials

A competitive atmosphere can bring out the best in dogs and their handlers. As certain aspects of protection work are seldom brought into practical use with many a dog, follow-up training can become sloppy or non-existent. Dogs and handlers therefore require refresher courses and they also require to be tested. Failure during an unexpected practical situation can be disastrous.

The police have their own district, regional and national trials as an incentive to higher standards of team work. The Royal Air Force have their own form of competition for the same reason. Civilian organised trials are run under the auspices of the Kennel Club and these are open to all dogs which are KC registered. Individual police forces play an active part in these civilian trials, with local handlers being members of most of the organising societies. These handlers give a great deal of their own time and help to ensure that these events are run on as practical a basis as possible.

The participation of police dog handlers as organisers, competitors and judges is important in all stakes but it is invaluable in ensuring the continuity of a realistic and practical background to the patrol work in the Police Dog Stakes.

Although civilian and police handlers make up the bulk of competitors the Prison Service, local authorities (parks security) and transport police also enter dogs and handlers from time to time.

However, working trials involve much more than protection work, which is covered by the Patrol Group of exercises within the Police Dog Stakes. Dogs require to be worked through each stage of competition and to gain qualifying marks before being permitted to progress. The top qualifications are those of Tracker Dog (Excellent) and Police Dog (Excellent). The appendix gives full coverage of the Kennel Club Working Trials Regulations.

This book covers only basic control and the training requirements for the Police Dog Patrol Group of exercises, but full training for the group of exercises such as Control, Agility and Nosework is given in *Training the German Shepherd Dog* (Pelham Books, 1977). This book is now recognised as an all-breed training manual for working trials and obedience tests. An in-depth knowledge of tracking and searching can be obtained from the *Nosework for Dogs* (Pelham Books, 1980).

Appendix

Kennel club working trial regulations

10th August, 1982

1. Management of Working Trials.—The management of a Working Trial shall be entrusted to a Working Trial Manager who shall be responsible for ensuring that the regulations are observed but he may not interfere with the Judges' decisions which shall be final.

The Working Trial Manager, appointed by the Committee of the Society holding the Trial, shall decide upon any matter not related to judging and not provided for in the Kennel Club Rules and Regulations for Working Trials and Obedience Classes and may call upon the Judge or Judges to assist with the decision which shall be final. The Working Trial Manager may not compete at the Trial and should be present throughout.

2. Judges.—When a Judge, from ill-health or any other unexpected cause, is prevented from attending or finishing a meeting, the Working Trial Manager once the Trial has commenced shall have the power of deciding what action is to be taken.

3. Schedule.—A Society holding a Working Trial must issue a schedule which is to be treated as a contract between the Society and the public and neither party is permitted to make any modification before the date of the Trial, except by permission of the Kennel Club, such alterations to be advertised in suitable publications where possible.

The schedule must contain:-
(*a*) The date and place of the Working Trial.
(*b*) The latest date for applying for entry at the Trial. A separate official entry form which must be an exact copy of the wording of the specimen entry form issued by the Kennel Club.
(*c*) The amounts of entry fees and any prize money.
(*d*) The conditions of the draw for the order of running.
(*e*) The conditions and qualifications for making entries and for intimating acceptance or refusal of entries.

(f) An announcement that the Working Trial is held under Kennel Club Working Trial Rules and Regulations with such exceptions and conditions as the Committee of the Society may decide. Such exceptions and conditions must have received the approval of the General Committee of the Kennel Club prior to publication of the schedule.

(g) The definition of each Stake, together with the qualification or limitations for entry in that Stake.

(h) The names of Judges. An announcement that if the entries in the Companion Dog Stake exceed 30, a Judge may be appointed to judge the Elementary Search and the competitors notified accordingly.

4. Assessing Weather Conditions.—The Working Trial Manager and the Judges should assess the weather conditions and should they consider the weather unfit for holding the Trials the commencement may be postponed until such time as is considered necessary for the Trials to be abandoned and the entry fees returned.

5. Handling of Dogs by Owner or his Deputy.—An owner or handler may handle the dog, but it must be one or the other; and once the dogs have commenced work an owner must not interfere with his dog if he has deputed another person to handle it.

6. Certification by Judge(s).—The Judge(s) shall certify on a form provided by the Kennel Club that in their opinion the Stake was held in accordance with the Schedule and Kennel Club Rules and Regulations.

7. Disqualification of Dogs.—A dog shall be disqualified by the Judges and removed from the ground if in their opinion it is:

(a) Unfit to compete by reason of sexual causes.

(b) Suffering from any infectious or contagious disease.

(c) Interfering with the safety or chance of winning of an opponent.

(d) Of such temperament or is so much out of hand as to be a danger to the safety of any person or other animal.

(e) Likely to cause cruelty to the dog if it continues in the Trial.

If a dog competes which has been exposed to the risk of any contagious or infectious disease during the period of six weeks prior to the Working Trial and/or if any dog shall be proved to be suffering at a Working Trial from any contagious or infectious disease, the owner thereof shall be liable to be dealt with under Rule 9 of the Kennel Club Rules for Working Trials and Obedience Classes.

8. Certificates.—The Judge or Judges shall give certificates at a Championship Working Trial PD (Police Dog), TD (Tracking Dog), WD (Working Dog), UD (Utility Dog), and CD (Companion Dog) Stake to those dogs which have obtained 70% or more marks in each group of exercises in the Stake entered (provided that the dog has complied with any additional requirements for that Stake). The added qualification 'Excellent' shall be awarded should the dog also obtain 80% or more marks of the total for the Stake.

Societies may issue these Qualification Certificates in Championship Stakes to their own design, subject to the approval of the Kennel Club but they must contain the name and breed of the dog, the name of the owner, the title of the Society and date of the Trials, the qualification and marks awarded and the signatures of the Judge and Working Trial Manager.

The Judge or Judges at Open Working Trials run to these schedules shall give Certificates of Merit for those dogs whose marks would have gained them a qualification 'Excellent' at a Championship Working Trial, provided that the Certificate contains the following words: 'This Certificate does not entitle the dog named thereon to any qualification recognised by the Kennel Club except entry in appropriate Stakes at Championship Working Trials'. Such Certificates of Merit must contain the name and breed of the dog, the name of the owner, the title of the Society and date of the Trial, the Stake and the marks awarded (without reference to any qualification) and the signatures of the Judge(s) and Working Trial Manager.

9. Prizes.—The winner of the Stake shall be the dog that has qualified with 70% or more marks in each group of the Stake and has obtained most marks. No dog that has not so qualified shall be placed in the prize list above a qualified dog. If no dog has qualified the dog with the highest number of marks may be awarded the prize. Judges are also empowered and instructed to withhold any prize or prizes if in their opinion the dogs competing do not show sufficient merit. Nothing in this Regulation shall apply to the award of 'Special' prizes.

10. Penalties for impugning the decisions of the Judges.—If anyone taking part in the Trials openly impugns the decision of the Judge or Judges, he is liable to be dealt with by the Committee under Rules 9 or 10 of the Kennel Club Rules for Working Trials and Obedience Classes.

11. Order of Running.—The order of running tracks shall be determined by a draw and competitors notified accordingly prior to the day of the Trial.

12. Disqualification for Absence.—The Working Trial Manager shall announce the specific time at which a dog or group of dogs may be called for any exercise or group of exercises. Each dog must be brought up at its proper time and in its proper turn without delay. If occasion demands the times and order may be changed at the discretion of the Working Trial Manager with the approval of the Judge or Judges, provided that no hardship is thereby caused to any competitor. If absent when called, the dog shall be liable to be disqualified by the Judge or Judges.

13. Method of Working.—The Judge or Judges in consultation with the Working Trial Manager may arrange for dogs to be working singly or together in any numbers. All dogs entered in a Stake shall be tested as far as possible under similar conditions.

14. Regulations Regarding Handling.
(*a*) A person handling a dog may speak, whistle or work it by hand signals as he wishes, but he can be called to order by the Judge or Judges for making

unnecessary noise, and if he persists in doing so the Judge or Judges can disqualify the dog.

(*b*) No person shall carry out punitive correction or harsh handling of a dog.

15. Awards.—All awards made by the Judge or Judges at a Working Trial shall be in accordance with the agreed scale of points approved by the General Committee of the Kennel Club. Equal awards for any of the prizes offered at a Working Trial are prohibited.

16. Notification of Awards.—The Secretary of a Working Trial shall send (within 7 days of the Trial) the Judges' certification and two marked catalogues to the Kennel Club indicating the prize winners and those dogs to which the Judges have awarded Certificates.

17. Entry Forms.—Entry Forms must be in accordance with the approved form which must be issued by the Secretary of the Working Trial, and all entries must be made thereon and not otherwise, and entirely in ink; only one person shall enter on one form. All such entry forms must be preserved by the Committee of a Working Trial meeting for at least twelve months from the last day of the Trial.

18. Refusal of Entries.—The Committee of any Meeting may reserve to themselves the right of refusing any entries on reasonable grounds.

19. Objections to Dogs.—An objection to a dog must be made to the Secretary in writing at any time within twenty-one days of the last day of the meeting upon the objector lodging with the Secretary the sum of £5.00. The deposit may be returned after the General Committee of the Kennel Club has considered the objection. Should any objection be made other than under Regulation 7(a) to 7(e) the dog should be allowed to compete and a full report made to the Kennel Club.

When an objection is lodged the Secretary of the Society must send to the Kennel Club:-

(*a*) A copy of the objection.

(*b*) The name and address of the objector.

(*c*) The name and address of the owner of the dog.

(*d*) All relevant evidence.

The objection will then be dealt with by the General Committee of the Kennel Club whose decision shall be final.

No objection shall be invalidated solely on the grounds that it was incorrectly lodged.

If the dog objected to be disqualified, the prize to which it would otherwise have been entitled shall be forfeited, and the dog or dogs next in order of merit shall move up and take the prize or prizes.

No spectator, not being the owner of a dog competing, or his accredited representative has the right to lodge any objection to a dog or to any action taken at the meeting unless he be a member of the Committee of the Society or of the General Committee of the Kennel Club or a Steward. Any objection so lodged will be disregarded.

20. Withdrawal of dogs from Competition.—No dog entered for competition and actually at the meeting, may be withdrawn from competition without notice to the Working Trials Manager. No dog shall compulsorily be withdrawn from a Stake by reason of the fact that it has obtained less than 70% of the marks in any one group.

21. Failure to Participate in Any Exercise.—Failure to participate in any exercise in a group in any Stake shall result in failure to qualify in that group.

22. The Working Trials and Obedience Committee shall issue an Appendix to the Schedule of Exercises and Points, 'Description of Exercises and Guidance for Judges and Competitors at Working Trials', which they may from time to time alter and in respect of which notice shall be given in the Kennel Gazette.

23. Working Trials for Bloodhounds shall be exempt from Working Trial Regulations 8, 9, 14(a), 15 and 21 and the Definitions of Stakes and Schedule of Exercises and Points. Until further notice the schedule of each Bloodhound Working Trial shall be submitted to the Kennel Club for approval before publication, in accordance with the provision of Rule 3 of the Kennel Club Rules for Working Trials and Obedience Classes.

Definitions of stakes

When entering for Championship or Open Working Trials, wins at Members Working Trials will not count.

No dog entered in P.D. or T.D. Stakes shall be eligible to enter in any other Stake at the meeting.

All Police dogs shall be considered qualified for entry in W.D. Championship Stakes if they hold the Regional Police Dog qualification 'Excellent', provided that such entries are countersigned by the Senior Police Officer I/C when such entries are made. Dogs holding this qualification are not eligible for entry in C.D. or U.D. Open or Championship Stakes, nor in W.D. Open Stakes.

No Working Trial Stake shall be limited to less than 30 dogs. If a limit is imposed on entries in any Stake, it shall be carried out by ballot after the date of closing of entries. Championship T.D. or P.D. Stakes shall not be limited by numbers in any way.

Open working trial

Companion Dog (C.D.) Stake.—For dogs which have not qualified C.D. Ex or U.D. Ex or won three or more first prizes in C.D. or any prize in U.D. Stakes, W.D. Stakes, P.D. or T.D. Stakes at Open or Championship Working Trials.

Utility Dog (U.D.) Stake.—For dogs which have not been awarded a Certificate of Merit in U.D., W.D., P.D. or T.D. Stakes.

Working Dog (W.D.) Stake.—For dogs which have been awarded a Certificate of Merit in U.D. Stakes but not in W.D., P.D. or T.D. Stakes.

Tracking Dog (T.D.)Stake.—For dogs which have been awarded a Certificate of Merit in W.D. Stakes but not in T.D. Stakes.

Police Dog (P.D.) Stake.—For dogs which have been awarded a Certificate of Merit in W.D. Stakes.

Championship working trial

Companion Dog (C.D.) Stake.—For dogs which have not won three or more first prizes in C.D. Stakes or any prize in any other Stake at Championship Working Trials.

Utility Dog (U.D.) Stake.—For dogs which have won a Certificate of Merit in an Open U.D. Stake. A dog is not eligible for entry in this Stake if it has been entered in the W.D. Stake on the same day.

Working Dog (W.D.) Stake.—For dogs which have qualified U.D. Ex and have won a Certificate of Merit in Open W.D. Stakes.

Tracking Dog (T.D.) Stake.—For dogs which have qualified W.D. Ex and have won a Certificate of Merit in Open T.D. Stakes.

Police Dog (P.D.) Stake.—For dogs which have qualified W.D. Ex.

Members' working trial

This is restricted to the members of the Society holding the Working Trial and eligibility for Stakes is as for Open Working Trials.

Judges at championship working trials

For C.D. Stake: Must have judged at least two Open Working Trials and have as a handler qualified a dog 'Excellent' in a Championship C.D. Stake.

For U.D. Stake: Must have judged U.D. or W.D. Stakes at two Open Trials, have judged C.D. Stake at a Championship Trial and have as a handler qualified a dog 'Excellent' in a Championship W.D. Stake.

For W.D. Stake: Must have judged U.D. or W.D. Stakes at two Open Trials, U.D. Stake at a Championship Trial and have as a handler qualified a dog 'Excellent' in a Championship W.D. Stake.

For P.D. Stake and T.D. Stake: Must have judged at two Open Trials, W.D. Stake at a Championship Trial and qualified a dog 'Excellent' in the Stake for which he was nominated to judge. There must be an interval of not less than six calendar months between appointments of the same judge for Championship T.D. and/or P.D. Stakes.

Note: Service and Police judges are eligible to judge U.D. Stake at a Championship Trial provided they have qualified a dog W.D. 'Excellent'. They must qualify for approval for other Stakes as above, except that those who have judged all parts at Regional or National Police Dog Trials will not have to qualify as a civilian handler.

Kennel Club Working Trial Championships

(*a*) The Kennel Club Working Trial Championships at which Police Dog (PD) and Tracking Dog (TD) Stakes shall be scheduled are held annually.

(*b*) The responsibility for organising the Championships each year will normally be delegated to a Working Trial Society approved to hold Championship Working Trials, such Society to be selected by the Working Trials and Obedience Committee from applications submitted by Societies. No Society to stage the event two years in succession.

(*c*) The Secretary of the Kennel Club will unless otherwise specified be the Working Trial Secretary for the event, the Society scheduling the Championships appointing a Trials Manager.

(*d*) The following shall be the method of selection of judges for the Championships:- Nominated by Working Trials Societies which have been granted Championship Working Trial status for ballotting by Working Trial Council, final selection by the Working Trials and Obedience Committee.

(*e*) Dogs eligible for entry in the Championships qualify as follows:-

(*i*) TD Championship: A dog must have been placed 1st in Championship TD Stake and qualified 'Excellent' in the Stake during the period 1st October-30th September preceding the Championships.

(*ii*) PD Championship: A dog must have been placed 1st in Championship PD Stake and qualified 'Excellent' in the Stake during the period 1st October-30th September preceding the Championships.

(*iii*) Dogs which qualify as above in both PD and TD Championship Stakes are permitted to be entered in either or both Championship Stakes.

(*iv*) The Winners of the previous year's Championship Stakes qualify automatically.

(*v*) No other dogs are eligible for entry in the Championships except by special permission of the General Committee of the Kennel Club.

(*f*) The Championships will normally be held during the third weekend in October each year.

(*g*) The winner of each Stake in the Championships is entitled to the description of Working Trial Champion provided it qualifies 'Excellent'.

(*h*) The Working Trial Society selected to hold the Championships is allowed to forgo one Open Working Trial during the same year.

Schedule of exercises and points

Companion dog (CD) stake		Marks	Group Total	Minimum Group Qualifying Mark
Group I. Control				
1 Heel on Leash		5		
2 Heel Free		10		
3 Recall to Handler		5		
4 Sending the dog away		10	30	21
Group II. Stays				
5 Sit (2 Minutes)		10		
6 Down (10 Minutes)		10	20	14
Group III. Agility				
7 Scale (3) Stay (2) Recall (5)		10		
8 Clear Jump		5		
9 Long Jump		5	20	14
Group IV. Retrieving and Nosework				
10 Retrieve a dumb-bell		10		
11 Elementary Search		20	30	21
	Totals	100	100	70

Utility dog (UD) stake		Marks	Group Total	Minimum Group Qualifying Mark
Group I. Control				
1 Heel Free		5		
2 Sending the dog away		10		
3 Retrieve a dumb-bell		5		
4 Down (10 Minutes)		10		
5 Steadiness to gunshot		5	35	25
Group II. Agility				
6 Scale (3) Stay (2) Recall (5)		10		
7 Clear Jump		5		
8 Long Jump		5	20	14
Group III. Nosework				
9 Search		35		
10 Track (95) Article (15)		110	145	102
	Totals	200	200	141

Working dog (WD) Stake		Marks	Group Total	Minimum Group Qualifying Mark
Group I. Control				
1 Heel Free		5		
2 Sending the dog away		10		
3 Retrieve a dumb-bell		5		
4 Down (10 Minutes)		10		
5 Steadiness to gunshot		5	35	25
Group II. Agility				
6 Scale (3) Stay (2) Recall (5)		10		
7 Clear Jump		5		
8 Long Jump		5	20	14
Group III. Nosework				
9 Search		35		
10 Track (90) Articles (10+10=20)		110	145	102
	Totals	200	200	141

Tracking dog (TD) stake		Marks	Group Total	Minimum Group Qualifying Mark
Group I. Control				
1 Heel Free		5		
2 Sendaway and Directional Control		10		
3 Speak on Command		5		
4 Down (10 Minutes)		10		
5 Steadiness to Gunshot		5	35	25
Group II. Agility				
6 Scale (3) Stay (2) Recall (5)		10		
7 Clear Jump		5		
8 Long Jump		5	20	14
Group III. Nosework				
9 Search		35		
10 Track (100) Article (10+10+10=30)		130	165	116
	Totals	220	220	155

Police dog (PD) stake	Marks	Group Total	Minimum Group Qualifying Mark
Group I. Control			
1 Heel Free	5		
2 Send away and Directional Control	10		
3 Speak on Command	5		
4 Down (10 Minutes)	10		
5 Steadiness to Gunshot	5	35	25
Group II. Agility			
6 Scale (3) Stay (2) Recall (5)	10		
7 Clear Jump	5		
8 Long Jump	5	20	14
Group III. Nosework			
9 Search	35		
10 Track (60) Articles (10 + 10 = 20)	80	115	80
Group IV. Patrol			
11 Quartering the Ground	45		
12 Test of Courage	20		
13 Search and Escort	25		
14a Recall from Criminal	30		
14b Pursuit and Detention of Criminal	30	150	105
Totals	320	320	224

Description of exercises and guidance for judges and competitors at working trials

A   Method of Handling.—Although implicit obedience to all orders is necessary, dogs and handlers must operate in as free and natural a manner as possible. Excessive formalism may be penalised, particularly if, in the opinion of the Judge, it detracts from the ability of the dog to exercise its senses in relation to all that is happening in the vicinity. Persistent barking, whining etc. in any exercise other than location of articles, person or speak on command should be penalised. Food may not be given to the dog by the handler whilst being tested.

B   Heel Work.—The Judge should test the ability of the dog to keep his shoulder reasonably close to the left knee of the handler who should walk smartly in his natural manner at normal, fast and slow paces through turns and among and around persons and obstacles. The halt, with the dog sitting to heel and a 'figure of eight' may be included at any stage.

Any act, signal or command or jerking of the leash which in the opinion of the Judge has given the dog unfair assistance shall be penalised.

C   Sit (2 Minutes).—Dogs may be tested individually or in a group or groups. The Judge or Steward will give the command 'last command' and handlers should then instantly give their final commands to the dogs. Any further commands or signals to the dogs will be penalised. Handlers will then be instructed to leave their dogs and proceed to positions indicated by the Judge or Steward until ordered to return to them. Where possible, such positions should be out of sight of the dogs but bearing in mind the short duration of the exercise this may not be practical. Dogs must remain in the sit position throughout the test until the Judge or Steward indicates that the test has finished. Minor movements must be penalised. The Judge may use his discretion should interference by another dog cause the dog to move.

D   Down (10 Minutes).—Handlers must be out of sight of the dogs who may be tested individually or in a group or groups. The Judge or Steward will give the command 'last command' and handlers should then instantly give their final commands to their dogs. Any further commands or signals to the dogs will be penalised. Handlers will then be instructed to leave their dogs and proceed to positions indicated by the Judge or Steward until ordered to return to them. Dogs must remain in the 'Down' position throughout the test until the Judge or Steward indicates that the test has finished. No dog will be awarded any marks that sits, stands or crawls more than its approximate body length in any direction. Minor movements must be penalised. The Judge may use his discretion should interference by another dog cause a dog to move. The Judge may test the dog by using distractions but may not call it by name.

E   Recall to Handler.—The dog should be recalled from the 'Down' or 'Sit' position. The handler being a reasonable distance from the dog at the discretion of the Judge. The dog should return at a smart pace and sit in front of the handler, afterwards going smartly to heel on command or signal. Handler to await command of the Judge or Steward.

F   Retrieve a Dumb-Bell.—The dog should not move forward to retrieve nor deliver to hand on return until ordered by the handler on the Judge's or Stewards' instructions. The Retrieve should be executed at a smart pace without mouthing or playing with the object. After delivery the handler will send his dog to heel on the instructions of the Judge or Steward.

G   Send Away and Directional Control.—The minimum distance that the Judge shall set for the Send Away shall be 20 yards for the CD Stake and 50 yards for all other Stakes. The TD and PD Stakes shall also include a redirection of a minimum of 50 yards. When the dog has reached the designated point or the Judge is satisfied that after a reasonable time the handler cannot improve the position of the dog by any further commands the dog should be stopped in either the stand, sit or down position at the discretion of the handler. At this point in the TD or PD Stakes the Judge or Steward shall instruct the handler to redirect his dog. In all Stakes, whilst the Judge should take into account the number of commands used during the exercise, importance should be placed upon the handler's ability to direct his dog to the place indicated.

H   Steadiness to Gunshot.—The most appropriate occasion for testing this exercise would be in open country. The dog may be either walking at heel free or be away from the handler who must be permitted to remain within controlling distance whilst the gun is fired. Any sign of fear, aggressiveness or barking must be penalised. This test shall not be carried out without prior warning, or incorporated in any other test. The Judge will not provoke excitement by excessive display of the gun, nor shall the gun be pointed at the dog.

I   Speak on Command.—The Judge will control the position of the handler in relation to the dog and may require the handler to work the dog walking at heel. If the dog is not required to walk at heel, the handler may at his discretion place the dog in the stand, sit or down. The dog will be ordered to speak and cease speaking on command of the Judge or Steward who may then instruct the handler to make the dog speak again. Speaking should be sustained by the dog whilst required with the minimum of commands and/or signals. Continuous and/or excessive incitements to speak shall be severely penalised. This test should not be incorporated with any other test.

J   Agility.—No part of the scale or clear or long jump equipment to be traversed by a dog shall be less than three feet wide nor be in any way injurious to the dog. The tests shall be followed in a sequence agreed by the Judge and will commence with the Scale. The Scale should be a vertical wall of wooden planks and may have affixed on both sides three slats evenly distributed in the top half of the jump. The top surface of the Scale may be lightly padded. The handler should approach the Scale at a walking pace and halt four to nine feet in front of it and in his own time order the dog to scale. On reaching the other side the dog should be ordered to stay in the stand, sit or down position, the handler having previously nominated such a position to the Judge. The Judge should ensure that the dog will stay steady and may indicate to the handler where he should stand in relation to his dog and the Scale before ordering the dog to be recalled over the Scale. A dog which fails to go over the Scale at the second attempt shall be excluded from the stay and recall over the Scale. Failure in the recall over the Scale does not disqualify from marks previously gained.

The handler may either approach the clear and long jumps with the dog or send it forward or stand by the jumps and call the dog up to jump. At no time should the handler proceed beyond any part of the jumps before they have been traversed by the dog. Once the dog has cleared the obstacle he should remain on the other side under control until joined by the handler. The clear jump should be so constructed that it will be obvious if the dog has exerted more than slight pressure upon it. The rigid top bar may be fixed or rest in cups and the space below may be filled in but the filling should not project above the bottom of the top bar. Appreciable pressure exerted by the dog on the clear jump shall be considered to be a failure. Casual fouling with fore or hind legs will be penalised at the discretion of the Judge. Failure or refusal at any of the three types of jump may be followed by a second attempt and any one such failure shall be penalised by at least 50% of the marks allotted to that part of the exercise in which the dog is given a second attempt.

Jumping heights and lengths:-

Companion dog (CD) stake and utility dog (UD) stake

(a) Scale

Dogs not exceeding 10 in. at shoulder	3 ft.
Dogs not exceeding 15 in. at shoulder	4 ft.
Dogs exceeding 15 in. at shoulder	6 ft.

(b) Clear Jump

Dogs not exceeding 10 in. at shoulder	1 ft. 6 in
Dogs not exceeding 15 in. at shoulder	2 ft.
Dogs exceeding 15 in. at shoulder	3 ft.

(c) Long Jump

Dogs not exceeding 10 in. at shoulder	4 ft.
Dogs not exceeding 15 in. at shoulder	6 ft.
Dogs exceeding 15 in. at shoulder	9 ft.

Working dog (WD) stake, tracking dog (TD) stake and police dog (PD) stake

(a) Scale	6 ft.
(b) Clear Jump	3 ft.
(c) Long Jump	9 ft.

K   Search.—The Companion Dog (CD) Stake Search shall contain three articles and all other Stakes shall contain four articles. In all Stakes fresh articles must be placed for each dog who must recover a minimum of two articles to qualify. As a guide the articles should be similar in size to a six inch nail or a match box, but the Judge should choose articles in relation to the nature of the ground and the Stake which he is judging. The time allotted shall be four minutes in the CD Stake and five minutes in all other Stakes. The articles should be well handled and placed by a Steward who shall foil the ground by walking in varying directions over the area. Each competitor shall have a separate piece of land.

The CD Stake search area shall be 15 yards square, all other Stakes being 25 yards square and shall be clearly defined by a marker peg at each corner. The handler may work his dog from any position outside the area, provided that he does not enter it.

In the CD Stake a maximum five marks should be allotted for each article and a maximum five marks for style and control. In all other Stakes a maximum seven marks should be allotted for each article and a maximum seven marks for style and control.

L   Track.—The track should be plotted on the ground to be used for the nosework by Stewards previous to the day of commencement of the Trials. An area of ground which has had a track laid over it must not have another track laid over it until the following day. The track shall be single line and may include turns. The articles should be in keeping with the nature of the ground. There shall be a marker left by the track layer to indicate the start of the track. In the UD Stake a second marker should be left not more than 30 yards from the start to indicate the direction of the first leg.

Unless the Judge considers the dog to have lost the track beyond recovery or has run out of the time allotted for the completion of the track a handler may recast his dog at his discretion. The Judge should not at any time indicate to the handler where he should recast his dog except in exceptional circumstances.

The track shall be approximately half a mile long and should be laid as far as possible by a stranger to the dog. The article(s) should be well scented. When the judging is in progress the track layer shall be present at the side of the Judge to indicate the exact line of the track and the position of the articles.

The UD Stake track shall be not less than half an hour old and shall include one article at the end, recovery of the article not being a requirement for qualification.

The WD and PD Stake tracks shall be not less than one and a half hours old and shall include two articles one of which must be recovered to qualify.

The TD Stake track shall be not less than three hours old and shall include three articles two of which must be recovered to qualify.

In all Stakes the last article shall indicate the end of the track. No two articles should be laid together.

A spare track additional to requirements should be laid but the opportunity to run a new track should be given only in exceptional circumstances.

The area used for Tracking is out of bounds to all competitors for practice Tracks and exercise from the time of the first track and any competitor found contravening this instruction is liable to be disqualified by the Judge and/or Stewards from participating in the Trial in accordance with the provision of Regulation No. 7(c).

The dog must be worked on a harness and tracking line.

M   Quartering the Ground.—The missing person or criminal should be protected to the minimum extent consistent with safety. He should remain motionless out of sight of the handler, but should be accessible on investigation to a dog which has winded him.

The Judge should satisfy himself that the dog has found the person and has given warning spontaneously and emphatically without being directed by the handler. Once the person has been detected and the dog has given voice, he may offer meat or other food which should be refused by the dog. If the dog ignores the food he may throw it on the ground in front of the dog. A dog which bites the person or criminal must be severely penalised.

N   Test of Courage.—This is a test of courage rather than of control. Dogs will not be heavily penalised in this test for lack of control. Handlers must be prepared to have the dog tested when on the lead by an unprotected Judge or Steward, and/or when off the lead by a protected Steward. The method of testing will be at the discretion of the Judge.

O   Search and Escort.—The criminal will be searched by the handler with the dog off the lead at the sit, stand or down. The Judge will assess whether the dog is well placed tactically and ready to defend if called to do so.

The handler will then be told to escort the prisoner(s) at least 30 yards in a certain direction, he will give at least one turn on the direction of the Judge. During the exercise the criminal will turn and attempt to overcome the handler. The dog may defend spontaneously or on command and must release the criminal at once both when he stands still or when the handler calls him off. The handler should be questioned as to his tactics in positioning the dog in both search and escort.

P   Recall from Criminal. (Exercise 14(a)).—The criminal, protected to the minimum extent consistent with safety, will be introduced to the handler whose dog will be free at heel. After an unheated conversation the criminal will run away. At a reasonable distance the handler will be ordered to send his dog. When the dog is approximately halfway between the handler and the criminal he will be ordered to be recalled. The recall may be by whistle or voice. The criminal should continue running until the dog returns or closes. If the dog continues to run alongside the criminal the criminal should run a further ten or dozen paces to indicate this.

Q   Pursuit and Detention of Criminal. (Exercise 14(b)).—The criminal (a different one for choice) and handler should be introduced as above, and the dog sent forward under the same conditions. The criminal must continue to attempt to escape and, if possible, should do so through some exit or in some vehicle once the dog has had a chance to catch up with him. The dog must be regarded as having succeeded if it clearly prevents the criminal from continuing his line of flight, either by holding him by the arm, knocking him over or close circling him till he becomes giddy. If the dog fails to make a convincing attempt to detain the criminal, it shall lose any marks that it may have obtained under exercise 14(a) or alternatively, it shall not be tested on exercise 14(a) if that follows exercise 14(b).

Index

acceptance of a presence, 32–3, 93–100
advertisements, 54–6
aggressiveness, 27
   alertness and, 31–2
   controlled, 104–11
agility, 131–2
alertness, 27, 30–1
Alsatians *see* German
   Shepherds
arm:
   gripping, 112–14
   protecting equipment, 113–14
arrest, power of, 62–3
attention, gaining, 74–5
attentiveness, 27
awareness of presence, 30–1, 90–1

barking, 70–1
   stopping, 93
   warning dogs, 23
   when required, 91–3
biting:
   failure to control, 46
   protection duties, 104–11
Bouvier Des Flandres, 41
breeders, moral responsibilities, 51–3
breeds, choice of, 37–41
buildings, searching, 128–9
Bull Terriers, 37
Bulldogs, 38
buying dogs, advertisements, 54–6

calling back, 75–7
car protection, 20, 23
caravans, protection, 20–1
championship working trials, 140–1
character, 27
characteristics, 26–30
   character, 27
   physique, 29

senses, 27
stature, 29
temperament, 27
check chain, 71
choice of dog, 37–41
choke chain, 71
clear jump, 131
collars, 71
Combi-collar, 71
communication, control training,
   69–71
confidence, 27
control:
   failure, 46–9
   handler's, 43–5
control training, 67–87
   basic principles, 69
   calling back, 75–7
   collars, 71
   communication, 69–71
   equipment, 71–3
   exercises, 74–87
   gaining attention, 74–5
   leads, 72
   loose lead walking, 77–80
   stay exercises, 80–7
Corgis, 38
courage, 36
   tests of, 114–16
Criminal Law Act (1967), 63
'criminals', protection equipment,
   113–14
   role of, 90
criminals *see* intruders
cross-breeds, 41

Dachshunds, 38
detecting presence, 33–4
detention of intruders, 117–20
deterrent, 37

dogs as, 23
disarming criminals, 116–17
distractions
    down-stay and, 86–7
    recall and, 75–7
Dobermanns, 38, 41
Dogs Act (1871), 61
Dogs Act (1906), 61
domestic situations, 20–1
    legal responsibilities, 61–2
    moral responsibilities, 51
doped food, 122–3
down-stay, 84–7

equipment:
    collars, 71
    leads, 72
    long lines, 73
escape, preventing, 35–6, 101, 103–4
escorting criminals, 120
exercises:
    calling back, 75–7
    control training, 74–87
    gaining attention, 74–5
    loose lead walking, 77–80
    stay, 80–7
    working trials, 145–9

failure to control, 46–9
feel, sense of, 29
food refusal, 122–3
friendliness, 27

gamekeepers, 21–2
gate signs, 56–60
Gazehound breeds, 29
German Shepherd Dogs, 38, 41, 46–9,
    50–1
Guard Dogs Act (1975), 53–4, 63–6
guarding duties, training, 88–102
guns, reactions to, 120–2

handlers:
    control, 43–5
    protection, 36
hearing, 27, 29, 97
hidden person, quartering for, 124–9
Hovawarts, 41
Hughes, Rosalie, 52–3

indicating source of, 34–5
intruders:
    acceptance of, 32–3, 93–100
    awareness of, 30–1, 90–1
    chasing, 117–20
    detecting, 33–4
    detention, 117–20
    disarming, 116–117
    escorting, 120
    indicating, 31–2, 90–1
    indicating source of, 34–5
    keeping at bay, 35, 100–2
    maintaining contact with, 35, 100–2
    objection to, 33
    preventing escape of, 35–6, 101,
        103–4
    pursuit, 117–20
    quartering for, 124–9
    searching for, 116
    self-defence, 36, 103–4

jumping, 131

Labrador Retrievers, 37–8
leads, 72
legal responsibilities, 61–6
long jump, 131
loose lead walking, 77–80

maintaining contact with, 35
manwork, 103–23
    controlled aggression, 104–11
    dangers of, 49–51
    detention, 117–20
    escorting, 120
    food refusal, 122–3
    gripping the arm, 112–14
    physical agitation, 114–16
    prevention of escape, 103–4
    pursuit, 117–20
    reaction to guns, 120–2
    self defence, 103–4
    tests of courage, 114–16
Mastiffs, 38
missing person, quartering for, 124–9
mongrels, 41
moral responsibilities, 43–60
    advertisements, 54–6
    breeder's, 51–3

dangers of manwork, 49–51
domestic guard dogs, 51
failure to control, 46–9
gate signs, 56–60
handler control, 43–5
operational dogs, 53–4

nervousness, 27, 32

observance, 27
operational situations, 21–2
    legal responsibilities, 62–6
    moral responsibilities, 53–4
owners, moral responsibilities, 43–60

park security, 22
physique, 29
poachers, 21–2
poisoned food, 122–3
presence:
    acceptance of, 32–3, 93–100
    awareness of, 30–1, 90–1
    detecting, 33–4
    indicating, 31–2, 90–1
    objection to, 33
protection duties, 103–23
    controlled aggression, 104–11
    detention, 117–20
    escorting, 120
    food refusal, 122–3
    gripping the arm, 112–14
    physical agitation, 114–16
    prevention of escape, 103–4
    pursuit, 117–20
    reaction to guns, 120–2
    self defence, 103–4
    tests of courage, 114–16
protectors, dogs as, 25
pursuit, 117–20

quartering, for hidden person, 124–9

recall:
    running, 119
    training, 75–7
Rhodesian Ridgebacks, 38
Rottweilers, 38–41, 52–3

running recall, 119

scale jump, 131
scenting, 27, 29, 97
searching for a person, 116–17, 124–9
    in buildings, 128–9
    in the open, 125–8
security dogs, 21
self defence, 36–7, 103–4
senses, 27
sex, dogs, 42
shyness, 33
sight, 29
sign language, 69–70
sit, 77, 79
sit-stay, 81–4
smell, sense of, 27, 29, 97
sounds, 27, 29, 97
source of presence, 34–5
Staffordshire Bull Terriers, 38
stand-stay, 80–81
stature, 29
stay-exercises, 80–7
    down-stay, 81–4
    sit-stay, 81–4
    stand-stay, 80–1

temperament, 27
Town Police Clauses Act (1847), 62
training:
    control, 67–87
    guarding duties, 88–102
    protection duties, 103–23
    quartering, 124–9
    versatility, 130–4
tug-of-war exercises, 105–11

versatility, 130–4
vibrations, 29, 97

walking, loose lead, 77–80
warning dogs, 23
water bailiffs, 21–2
Wire-haired Fox Terriers, 38
working trials, 133–4
    championship, 140–1
    exercises, 145–9
    regulations, 135–41